DATE DUE

BURSTING BONDS

Blacks in the Diaspora

Darlene Clark Hine, John McCluskey, Jr., and David Barry Gaspar
General Editors

William Pickens at age 50. Photo
courtesy of William Pickens III.

BURSTING BONDS

ENLARGED EDITION

THE HEIR OF SLAVES

The Autobiography of a "New Negro"

BY

WILLIAM PICKENS

Edited by
William L. Andrews

INDIANA UNIVERSITY PRESS

Bloomington and Indianapolis

The paper used in this publication meets the minimum requirements of American
National Standard for Information Sciences—Permanence of Paper for Printed
Library Materials, ANSI Z39.48-1984.
∞™

Manufactured in the United States of America

Library of Congress Cataloging-in-Publication Data

Pickens, William, 1881–1954.
  Bursting bonds : the heir of slaves / by William Pickens ; edited
by William L. Andrews. — Enl. ed.
      p.   cm.
  ISBN 0-253-34496-4 (alk. paper) ; ISBN 0-253-20671-5 (pbk. : alk.
paper)
    1. Pickens, William, 1881–1954.   2. Afro-Americans—Biography.
3. National Association for the Advancement of Colored People—
Biography.   4. Southern States—Race relations.   5. Afro-Americans—
History—1877–1964.   I. Andrews, William L., date.   II. Title.
E185.97.P592   1991
973'.0496073—dc20   91-6847

1 2 3 4 5   95 94 93 92 91

CONTENTS

FOREWORD

by Benjamin L. Hooks

Any honor roll of those who contributed to the civil rights movement would have a high and honored place for the name of William Pickens.

Pickens's life belies the all-too-prevalent notion that Americans of African descent merely sat about waiting for the 1950s and 1960s to dawn before they became active in the quest for freedom. There was a civil rights movement years before the events usually described under that all-embracing name. William Pickens was among its guiding spirits. Some have called him a beacon light.

This marvelous man was a graduate of Yale University, taking his degree *summa cum laude* in 1904, and earning the cherished Phi Beta Kappa key along the way. He became the first black to win a major Yale prize when he won the first place award in the Ten Eyck Oratorical Contest of 1903. He also was the first black to be chosen a member of the Philosophical Oration Group at graduation.

In the era's raging debate between Booker T. Washington and W. E. B. Du Bois, Pickens cast his lot with Du Bois and became a member of the Niagara Movement, a precursor of the National Association for the Advancement of Colored People. Later, those who founded the NAACP enlisted Pickens's skill in their effort to develop the Association as a major force in civil rights. Pickens eventually became Assistant Director of Branches.

We of the NAACP know that "Dean" Pickens was one of those hardy spirits who saw to it that our foundation was well and truly laid. Pickens helped the organization, which could have been little more than a debating society for intellectuals, become a viable "grass-roots" movement. The NAACP reached out and touched the masses in large measure because William Pickens possessed a rare ability to "walk with kings nor lose the common touch." The capacity to be a bridge between the Ph.Ds and the no Ds remains one of the NAACP's greatest strengths.

For that gift, we and all America are greatly in the debt of William Pickens.

ACKNOWLEDGMENTS

I would like to thank William Pickens III for his generous help in the preparation of this edition of his grandfather's autobiography. My gratitude goes also to my research assistant, Daniel Murtaugh, for his contribution to this edition. The General Research Fund of the Office of Research, Graduate Studies, and Public Service of the University of Kansas provided additional support.

William L. Andrews

INTRODUCTION

by William L. Andrews

When *Bursting Bonds* was first published in August of 1923, its author, William Pickens, was a nationally recognized African American leader, one of the half-dozen best-known black men of his time. He had made a name for himself initially in 1904 as a Phi Beta Kappa graduate of Yale where his prize-winning oratory won him a lucrative offer from a New York speaker's bureau to undertake a three-year lecture tour of the United States.[1] Choosing instead to return to his native South, Pickens devoted himself to an academic career that took him from a position as professor of languages at Talladega College in Alabama in 1904 to the vice-presidency of Morgan College (now Morgan State University) in Baltimore in 1918. Pickens's considerable skill as a platform speaker made him an invaluable fund-raiser for the colleges with which he was associated and gave him a reputation in the black South as one of the up-and-coming men of his race. His writing gravitated toward political controversy and social criticism. As early as 1906 Pickens served notice that he stood for nothing less than full "equality, industrial, social and political" for black Americans, regardless of how reckless or radical this position might seem to the conservatives, black as well as white, of the South. Realizing that he was living during a turning point in African American history, Pickens at the age of twenty-five dedicated himself to write a "frank discourse" that would "force the wavering and faint-hearted to consider and choose principles" rather than remain "contemptible, Janus-faced, amphibological 'straddlers.' "[2]

His increasingly public espousal of the sociopolitical philosophy of men like W. E. B. Du Bois led Pickens to join the National Association for the Advancement of Colored People as one of its founding members in 1910 and to serve as one of its most effective early southern representatives. After the United States entered World War I, Pickens worked with others in the NAACP to ensure that, for the first time, black men as well as white would be trained for the army's officer corps. By 1917, he had decided that his talents and ambitions fitted him better for the life of a civil rights activist than that of a college administrator.

In 1919, Pickens's associates in the inner circle of the NAACP agreed
and offered him the position of assistant to James Weldon Johnson,
the highly respected field secretary of the association. Scarcely more
than a year later, after Johnson became the first African American to
head the NAACP as executive secretary, Pickens was appointed to
associate field secretary, a post he shared with Mrs. Addie W. Hunton.
Barely forty years old at the time of this promotion, the self-described
"heir of slaves" must have felt considerable pride when he surveyed the
fifteen years of successful striving that had taken him from junior instructor at a small black southern college to senior official in the North's
most notable and influential civil rights organization. On the eve of
the 1920s, the decade of the "New Negro Renaissance," no black
American could lay better claim to the title of "New Negro" than
William Pickens.

Although it is commonplace to associate the term "New Negro" with
the cultural and artistic movement celebrated by Alain Locke in *The
New Negro* (1925), there is ample evidence of the currency of the term
among black intellectuals and pundits since the turn of the century.[3]
Two books, one published under the auspices of Booker T. Washington
and the other written by William Pickens, are chiefly responsible for
introducing the idea of a New Negro to the general readership of twentieth-century America. In 1900 Washington, aided by N. B. Wood
and Fannie Barrier Williams, fashioned *A New Negro for a New Century*,
a compendium of brief histories, biographies, and journalistic sketches
by various hands aimed at providing, in the words of the volume's
subtitle, "An Accurate and Up-to-Date Record of the Upward Struggles
of the Negro Race."[4] In 1916 William Pickens published *The New
Negro: His Political, Civil and Mental Status*, a collection of his own
essays dedicated to the "essential humanity and justice" of "the white
and the black men of tomorrow."[5] While Washington's volume was
concerned with proving how far the African American had come since
slavery, Pickens's allotted more space to the distance between what
blacks deserved as American citizens and what they had been forced
to accept. Far from pessimistic in tone, Pickens's *The New Negro* recalled with pride the achievements of blacks since emancipation and
looked forward to "the establishment of Universal Human Brother-
hood" throughout the civilized world (70). But he was convinced that
social and economic progress would not come without agitation, which
placed the onus on black people not merely to bear up under their

oppression but to combat it. "Those who have rights to acquire must be aggressive" (100), Pickens affirmed. "No people ever acquired rights by sitting down and waiting for them. Rights never come—calamities come—rights, you must go and get them" (101).

The fundamental right Pickens demanded for blacks in *The New Negro* was "full citizenship," by which he meant an end to all forms of segregation and a guarantee of the right to vote freely in local, state, and national elections. What stood in the way of these civil rights was, in Pickens's analysis, primarily white prejudice fed on ignorance and baseless fear. Pickens believed that he could do much to advance the cause of racial justice by enlightening whites who, because of segregation, knew little about the aspirations of the younger generation of African Americans like himself. Pickens believed that, in the absence of real contact with black people, most whites were "very slow to revise their ideals as to what constitutes a 'good' Negro. . . . It is difficult for them to conceive of an independent, self-respecting, self-directing Negro as good" (236). To Pickens it was precisely this common bias among whites against the "intelligent and aspiring Negro" that had become "our great stumbling block" (237). By explaining and justifying the social, economic, and political priorities of "the intelligent and aspiring Negro," the author of *The New Negro* hoped his book would teach whites to regard the African American "as a personality," not merely "a commodity" or "a utility" (238), as a "co-worker" with whites, no longer an "instrument" of them (174).

In *Bursting Bonds*, Pickens turned to autobiography to confirm the prediction he had made seven years earlier about the New Negro, namely, that he was "beginning to insist that he must be regarded first as a man and only incidentally as a usable article" (238). To introduce the New Negro "as a man," *Bursting Bonds* offered the white American reader the first self-portrait of a New Negro as an individual. Putting aside the essayistic discourse of his earlier book, in which he too "utilized" the New Negro as the object of sociopolitical inquiry, Pickens made a crucial and innovative decision in 1923 to personalize the New Negro. In and through his own life and his own voice, he would represent himself as the "independent, self-respecting, self-directing Negro" whom he had outlined in the abstract for the readers of *The New Negro*. In the process Pickens inaugurated an era of modern black autobiography that came to full articulation in the memoirs of such famous New Negroes as James Weldon Johnson, Langston Hughes, and Zora

Neale Hurston. Ten years before Johnson's *Along This Way* and almost two decades before *The Big Sea* (1940) and *Dust Tracks on a Road* (1942), *Bursting Bonds* forecast the trajectory of many a New Negro's early career; indeed, more than any other African American autobiography of the early twentieth century, it might accurately have been subtitled "The Making of a New Negro."

In one of the more remarkable distillations of New Negro conscious-ness in *Bursting Bonds*, Pickens wrote: "Life forced upon me, or de-veloped within me, the habit of thinking for myself, so that I have never been afraid to stand alone,—too little afraid perhaps. I have never had a disposition to imitate any authority, either in writing an essay, making a speech, getting a lesson into a pupil,—or sketching an autobiography."[6] An early historian of African American auto-biography challenged Pickens's claim to intellectual independence, however, charging that *Bursting Bonds* "bears the indelible mark of Booker T. Washington."[7] To the extent that this is true, it could hardly have been otherwise. After its publication in 1901, *Up from Slavery*, Washington's enormously popular and influential life story, became a virtual touchstone for black autobiography in succeeding decades, es-pecially in the eyes of whites. Washington engendered an entire school of autobiographers in his own image, men and women who saw in the pattern of the Tuskegeean's life and the politics of his example an instructive model for their own attempts at self-publication and pro-motion.[8] A young man like William Pickens, who had been born in the South under circumstances similar to those of Washington's early life, who had likewise pulled himself up by his own bootstraps to attain his ideal of an education, and who had chosen to devote himself to the uplift of his people in a college in the Tuskegeean's home state, could not help but evoke comparisons to the most famous black man of his time. Recalling his first meeting with Washington en route to joining the older man on the rostrum of the 1900 convention of the American Missionary Association, Pickens noted that the Tuskegeean "treated me with such kindly consideration that I was asked by pas-sengers if I was not Mr. Washington's son" (34). But it is significant that Pickens did not record what he thought or said in response. Instead he let this instance of mistaken affiliation stand as a subtle warning to the reader of *Bursting Bonds* not to mistake the parallels between his life and Washington's for an identification of the aspiring youth with the example set by his predecessor.

Distancing himself from Washington and all he stood for was demanding and somewhat dangerous for a young southern black man like Pickens. Upon graduation from Yale, he had received an invitation to teach at Tuskegee, partly as a tribute to his academic achievements but most likely because he had hewed to the Washington line in his undergraduate speeches and writing.[9] By opting to return to Talladega College, his alma mater, rather than become part of the Tuskegee machine, Pickens took his first step toward independence. Less than two years later, readers of *The Voice of the Negro*, a progressive black journal of opinion, discovered Pickens demanding in an essay bluntly entitled "Choose!" that "every intelligent and self-respecting Negro" take an unequivocal, public stand with regard to the philosophy and tactics of Washington on the one hand or Du Bois on the other. Although Pickens never identified the choice as between two men, but rather between two ideologies, no reader of *The Voice of the Negro* could have mistaken the writer's disgust with Washingtonian conservatism, which is characterized in "Choose!" as a cynical materialism that sacrifices civil rights and personal dignity in exchange for the chance to pursue, first and foremost, "the almighty dollar." The alternative for the courageous, Pickens stated, is dedication to principle at all costs, recognizing that full citizenship and equality of opportunity are the *desiderata* of the only meaningful and respectable success black people could ever have in America.

In light of the essays Pickens wrote for *The Voice of the Negro* from 1904 to 1906, and considering his endorsement of and participation in most of the civil rights conferences and groups that led up to the founding of the NAACP in 1910, one might be puzzled by his noncommittal treatment of Washington in *Bursting Bonds*. Pickens's refusal to attack the sage of Tuskegee directly was both strategic and necessary, however, given the almost unqualified reverence in which Washington's memory was held in white America during the decade after his death. Moreover, in 1911 Pickens had published the first installment of his autobiography under the title of *The Heir of Slaves*, in which he had taken care to portray his relationship to Washington as cordial, though not close.[10] *The Heir of Slaves*, which would become the first nine chapters of *Bursting Bonds*, seems to have been designed to evoke the myth—not to mention the title—of *Up from Slavery* partly in deference to a tried and true method of enhancing the image of an unfamiliar Negro in the eyes of his white audience. Thus, although by

1911 Pickens had identified himself with the NAACP as opposed to the conservative Bookerites, he chose not to give a hint of his civil rights activism in the latter pages of *The Heir of Slaves*, preferring to bring his story to a climax with an account of his winning the Henry James Ten Eyck Oratorical Contest at Yale. Moreover, in the "Afterword" to his 1911 autobiography, Pickens deliberately echoed Washington in pointing out how he too had rejected a chance to cash in on his notoriety as an orator after graduation from college in favor of returning to teach in the South, where he found "a greater field of usefulness to a Negro than any other profession" (42). Pickens went on, in language reminiscent of *Up from Slavery*, to express his thankfulness for "the blessing of a boyhood that trains to endurance and struggle" (43). In these ways Pickens showed that he would not hesitate to portray himself as following in Washington's footsteps, equally dedicated to "usefulness" and racial uplift, whenever he found the Tuskegeean's precedent adaptable to his own ends.

Nevertheless, one does not have to be particularly acute to discover that even as *The Heir of Slaves* seems to conform to the outline and goals of Washington's life, the narrative voice of Pickens's first autobiography refuses to echo the carefully modulated, consistently circumspect, unfailingly earnest and sincere tone that is the hallmark of *Up from Slavery* and one of the major reasons for its appeal among Washington's white contemporaries. Instead, the tone of *The Heir of Slaves*, while sometimes flattened out and deadpan in the Washington manner, takes on at other times a certain tense and edgy obliqueness bordering on insinuation, as if to push the reader beyond what is actually said to an implicit but for some reason unstatable conclusion. On still other occasions, a distinctly un-Washingtonian irony breaks through the narration in what might be called asides to the reader that reveal suppressed resentments and a desire to unloose a satiric wit. One has the feeling by the end of *The Heir of Slaves* that something is being alternately disclosed and withheld, as though the narrator is not entirely sure just how freely he should speak and how much of himself he should reveal to his reader. The hard-hitting five chapters added to *The Heir of Slaves* to make *Bursting Bonds* indicate that by 1923 Pickens felt ready to burst the bonds that restrained his utterance in 1911. Still it is important to remember that the author entitled *Bursting Bonds* an "enlarged edition of *The Heir of Slaves*" and reprinted the former text verbatim in the second autobiography. This decision suggests that while Pickens wanted

Bursting Bonds to climax with the arrival of the New Negro à la William Pickens on the social and cultural scene, he was also committed to preserving a record of himself in a crucially liminal stage of his career as a writer, when he was struggling with his own anxieties of influence and trying to find a way to speak for himself on his own literary authority.

William Pickens's account of his rise from virtually the lowest rung on the South's socioeconomic ladder to Phi Beta Kappa graduate of Yale University and eventually field secretary of the NAACP is both a great American success story and a classic African American ascent narrative. One of the reviewers of *Bursting Bonds* compared its author to Benjamin Franklin while another dubbed the story of his "determined progress" from the many disadvantages of his birth to the distinctions he attained at Yale "a minor American saga."[11] In the tradition of the American self-made man Pickens invited his reader to join him in savoring "delicious chapters of hard and profitable experience" from the story of his life (24). From the pinnacle of his Yale triumphs, he offered his reader the kind of advice typical of America's apostles of success at the turn of the century: "To do the best one can, wherever placed, is a summary of all the rules of success" (43). It is important to remember, however, that Pickens's variation on the self-made man theme is steeped in racial awareness and an abiding sense of the peculiar social significance of a black man's achieving success in the fields in which this black man so craved it. Pickens's single-minded desire for and almost obsession with intellectual excellence can be best understood against the background of his predecessors in African American autobiography who rose from slavery in the South to success in the North by virtue of an all-consuming belief that knowledge would make them free.

According to Robert B. Stepto, the narrative of ascent, one of the fundamental genres of black American literature, has its origins in the antebellum slave narrative, in which "an 'enslaved' and semi-literate figure" sets out on a journey to the North in search of freedom and opportunity. Most fugitive slaves concluded their ascent narratives with their arrival in the so-called free states, a victory signaled by some sort of autobiographical declaration of a new self endowed with the insights and powers of literacy. It is hard to overestimate the political significance of the acquisition of literacy to the protagonist of the nineteenth-century slave narrative. As Henry Louis Gates has pointed out, a wide-spread assumption in post-Enlightenment European thought was that writing "stood alone among the fine arts as the most salient repository of 'genius,' the visible sign of reason itself." Once a discerning slave like the young Frederick Douglass heard from his master that "learning would *spoil* the best nigger in the world" and would "forever unfit him to be a slave," the conclusion came naturally that the ability to read and write would open up the pathway to freedom. "Truly has it been said that, 'knowledge is power,' " wrote Austin Steward, who spoke for many of his fellow ex-slave autobiographers in predicating respect-able status and moral authority in the world of freedom on intellectual achievement and the ability to display it through the spoken and written word. This faith in "the ideal of 'book-learning' " sustained the masses of southern blacks well beyond the post-Reconstruction era, W. E. B. Du Bois argued, and remained the key to the creation of a leadership class of African Americans that would serve as an example to blacks and whites alike of the great value and potential of the Negro in the United States.[12]

Like many children of former slaves, William Pickens grew up in an atmosphere of profound reverence for learning. His parents' dedication to the education of their children was a major factor in their decision, early in Pickens's boyhood, to move from rural South Carolina to the towns of Pendleton and Seneca, where the school term for blacks was longer and not interrupted by the demands of the share-cropping economy. One of the notable features of the early part of *Bursting Bonds* is its emphasis on the conflict between the Pickens family's economic advancement and its educational fulfillment. The Pickenses' emigration westward to Arkansas in 1888 in search of better wages was by no means unusual at a time when the entire South was witnessing significant losses of its black farm laboring class to the Midwest. The family's subsequent reduction to what is bluntly termed "a state of debt-slavery" in *Bursting Bonds* has been called a classic case of a new form of bondage created in the post–Civil War South to keep blacks in subjection. Not only were the economic consequences of Jacob Pickens's "debt-slavery" devastating, but the necessity of keeping the children out of school in order to help overcome the debt demoralized the family and undermined its ultimate goals. For these reasons the Pickens family relocated yet again, this time to the environs of Little Rock. Explaining what mo-tivated his family's odyssey, Pickens quietly but firmly took issue with

Booker T. Washington's well-known critique of urban influences on blacks and his often-invoked idealization of rural life. "This move city-ward," Pickens stressed, "was not prompted, as is usually charged in such cases, by any desire to get away from work, but by the high motives of education and the future" (12).[13]

In the town of Argenta across the river from Little Rock, William Pickens got his long-delayed "real start in school." Chapters 3 through 5 of *Bursting Bonds* recount a series of academic successes that carried Pickens through high school to graduation in 1899 as class valedictorian. Although Pickens professed to have been "deeply in love with school and study," so much so that he preferred learning his lessons to playing with his siblings, a reader will look in vain in *Bursting Bonds* for details about what young Pickens actually studied and why he loved it so much. More prominent are schoolroom scenes of intense competition in which only martial terms can convey the import of the black youth's struggle to distinguish himself intellectually. From the outset of his career, "I had to fight my way on the playground as well as in the classroom" (13); entering high school, Pickens recalled having been "attacked first in one subject, then in another" by his own classmates (18). Looking back on the most dangerous of the jobs he took to help him finance his education, Pickens designated "the tyrant" with whom he worked as "one of my appointed teachers" and "benefactors" even though "he tried for weeks and weeks to knock my brains out" (21). The rough tutelage of Dink Jeter reinforced in his young pupil a conviction that every day would bring "a *contest* in which it was 'up to me' to win" (22). No wonder, therefore, that Pickens portrayed himself throughout his youth as assiduously seeking arenas in which to contest his abilities against those of his peers, first black and later white, who stood between him and the distinction he desired and deserved. From his early struggles to best his public school classmates to his bold decision to win the Henry James Ten Eyck Oratorical Contest at Yale, this "heir of slaves" had something to prove. More than just a test of his mettle and abilities, life seemed to this young black man a *contest* in which he could assert himself as a man only by competing literally head-to-head with any and all challengers.

Unlike conventional success stories marked by a complacent self-centeredness, *Bursting Bonds* shows that much more than personal reasons motivated William Pickens's youthful ambitions. Pickens hoped that by beating whites at their own academic game his example would

prove that blacks had capacities for intellectual success at least equal
to those of the more favored race. The problem was getting whites to
rethink their prejudices about what blacks were capable of in the classroom and in life. Some of Pickens's best irony appears in his treatment
of the white Arkansas lawyers who debate in his presence whether he
would profit by a college education, while "never addressing or noticing
me," as though he were nothing more than a "machine whose qualities
and capacities were the subject of discussion" (24). This experience of
objectification, in which a black achiever is not so much congratulated
and encouraged as treated like a freak of nature for whites to wonder
at and be amused by, recurs throughout the first nine chapters of *Bursting
Bonds*. No matter how well he does and how often he takes the first
prize, even after he wins the oratorical contest at Yale, Pickens recalls
that his Yale peers "never quite got away from the surprise that 'you
do your lessons as well as anybody!' " (41). Without depreciating the
"generous and manly enthusiasm" that many of his fellow students at
Yale expressed when he won the Ten Eyck prize, Pickens records the
snubs and resentments, the quiet effort to deny him entry into Phi Beta
Kappa, that also marked his ostensible arrival at the apex of his ambition. At the culmination of his Yale career, it is clear that despite
all the successes he amassed, Pickens had to recognize that he had not
truly arrived at a place where he could rest on his laurels; he would
have to continue to "push forward the front of [his] battle" (43) toward
ever-renewing struggles that had to be won.

Putting the best face on it, Pickens termed this ceaseless battle "inspiriting" and a "blessing." But it was a burden too, and an inescapable
one at that. With a candor rare among his predecessors in African
American success stories, Pickens acknowledged that a sense of the
relentless expectations of blacks as well as the conceit and condescen-
sion of whites fueled his all-consuming, near-obsessive drive for excellence. In a typically understated anecdote in chapter 9, we read that
early in his black public school experience Pickens had to learn a painful
lesson: "the man who succeeds is never conceded the right to fail" (44).
In light of this, one can see how every proof Pickens gave to whites
that blacks *could* succeed also exacted from him a heightened obligation
to blacks *never* to fail. In addition to helping to explain the mix of
anxiety and ambition that molded this New Negro, Pickens's revelation
of his sense of double duty sheds further light on the idea of "double-

consciousness" that Du Bois made the *sine qua non* for understanding the modern African American.[14]

Had Pickens published no more of his story than that which he incorporated into *The Heir of Slaves*, his place in the history of African American autobiography would probably rest on the fact that his text reads like a re-voicing of Douglass's *Narrative* followed by a coda that echoes *Up from Slavery*. The climax of Douglass's famous ascent narrative, featuring the ex-slave's discovery of his voice and mission on the abolitionist platform, established the precedent for the twentieth-century black's triumphal reception into Yale's "democratic community" after winning the Ten Eyck oratorical prize. But unlike Douglass in 1845, whose platform success earned him an honorable career as a social activist, Pickens in 1911 knew that he could not pursue mere "show-lecturing" without sacrificing his self-respect. Consequently, like Booker T. Washington, he dedicated himself to the education of his own people in the South. The end of *The Heir of Slaves* thus records the descent of its protagonist to the world from which he came, a reversal of the pattern of his life that the narrator, from the standpoint of seven years' experience as a teacher at Talladega, judged to have been "logical and good." This conclusion articulates the self-effacing ideal traditionally espoused by African American intellectuals as diverse as Du Bois and Washington. But was it an idealism that could sustain a person as self-assertive and combative, particularly when his rights and personal principles were at stake, as William Pickens? Partly in response to this question and partly to explain how the trajectory of his life had eventually reversed itself again, taking him out of the South and back to the North, Pickens composed the final installment of his autobiography in 1923.

Looking back on what he had written in 1911, Pickens introduced the new chapters of his autobiography by hinting at the limitations of his previous perspective. He portrayed the author of *The Heir of Slaves* as too inexperienced in "the battle of real life," too much wedded to the idealism of his undergraduate days. In the dozen years between 1911 and 1923, Pickens felt he had received a new and chastening education in "real living." He had learned from bitter experience that all too often even liberal and conscientious whites were put off by "a really straight-out, straight-up, manly and self-respecting Negro" (50). Yet this was precisely the way Pickens intended to portray himself and address his reader in the new chapters of his autobiography. Although he did not go so far as to label himself in 1923 a "New Negro," the tone, style, and focus of attention in the final chapters of his autobiography demonstrate conclusively enough who William Pickens had become.

At the end of *The Heir of Slaves*, Pickens pictured his first seven years at Talladega as wholly fulfilling. But the first chapter of the material he added in 1923 places his Talladega years in a much different light. Chapter 10 of *Bursting Bonds* provides its reader a rare glimpse into the inner workings of power in those colleges in the South, such as Talladega, that had been founded by whites for the education of blacks. As Pickens makes clear, because Talladega was literally a "missionary enterprise" (founded by the American Missionary Association), its control lay not in its on-site administration and faculty but rather in boards of trustees composed of New Yorkers and New Englanders who had little first-hand knowledge of the institution at all. To make informed policy decisions, the boards of such institutions relied on college presidents, generally white men, who themselves had so little direct contact with the faculty and students of their institutions that they had to depend on black subordinates for their own knowledge. Pickens attacked this system of white control of black higher education in the South for its obvious paternalism based on the assumption that blacks were not capable of directing the affairs of their own educational institutions. Pickens highlighted this problem by pointing to his own example as a case in point of what happens when a trained and qualified black man is hired by a school that prefers to promote only a "Negro of a usable type" (48), i.e., one willing to be managed by and for the interests of his white superiors.

Readers of today will wonder what turn of events caused Pickens to conclude that his superiors had come to see him as a Negro "paid to act, but too active to please; hired to do, but who *does too much*" (49). Pickens's biographer suggests that his activities on behalf of the fledgling NAACP—speaking engagements and recruiting efforts that sometimes took him away from his classes—irritated leading figures in the American Missionary Association. There is also evidence that the president of Talladega thought Pickens was partly responsible for a strike called by the student body in the spring of 1914 to demand more black faculty and a black administration. Add to this Booker T. Washington's be-

hind-the-scenes complaints to Pickens's superiors about what the Tuskegeean saw as the professor's "demagoguery," and one can easily see
how Pickens's brand of activism became "too much" for whites accus-
tomed to blacks who consistently deferred to their authority.[15] Although one might wish that Pickens had been explicit about many
more details in his exposé of the politics of Talladega, he had good
reason for not naming names. In addition to legal considerations, it
would not have been in the best interests of the NAACP for its field
secretary to attack publicly the leadership of a prominent black southern
college. Besides, Pickens had already gone farther than any black autobiographer before him in unmasking the mystique of power and paternalism in the black colleges of the South.

Pickens's discussion of his ten years at Talladega introduces the key
theme of the last four chapters of *Bursting Bonds*: what a New Negro
must be prepared to risk in the name of self-respect, independence,
and equality. At Talladega, Pickens had to make a decision similar to
that which he demanded of his *Voice of the Negro* readers in his essay
"Choose!" That is, he himself had to choose between personal security
and personal principle, between his status on the college faculty and
his standing in his own eyes. Rather than sacrifice the standards by
which he had measured and challenged himself for so long, Pickens
suggests that he preferred to forsake the blandishments of material success and security. The farther one goes in *Bursting Bonds*, the more
fundamental and dangerous the choices become for Pickens. In the two
most exciting chapters of his autobiography, "Wiley University and
Texas" and "Arkansas Traveler," Pickens pictures himself in the most
desperate contests of his life, pitting his convictions, his courage, and
his wits against naked southern racism, "a terror which unceasingly
denies [blacks] the primary recognition and the elemental expression
of self-respect" (58). The account of his verbal showdown with a white
Texan in chapter 12 and the story of his solitary challenge to Arkansas's
Jim Crow railroad statutes confirm through his own example what Pickens maintained in the concluding lines of *The New Negro*, namely,
that the New Negro "is resolved to fight, and live or die, on the side
of God and the Eternal Verities."

Pickens's reconstruction of these episodes illustrates in taut and sus-
penseful prose how the most mundane of matters, such as the payment
of a small debt by a white man to a black man, could erupt into an
explosive scene of violence and potential tragedy. It is extremely un-

usual in African American autobiography of the late nineteenth or early twentieth centuries to find such close attention as Pickens gives to incidents of individual conflict between a black man and whites who seek to intimidate him into submission to the Jim Crow order. In the twenty years between *Up from Slavery* and *Bursting Bonds*, the most widely read black autobiographies, written by the most popular and conventionally successful African Americans, noted general improvements on the southern racial scene and tactfully elided comments about personal insults received at the hands of southern racism. In a bold and unapologetic break with the literary etiquette of African American autobiography of his time, Pickens made clear that his aim in writing about his experiences in Texas and Arkansas was "to tell the whole truth" about "the unhappy situation and savage treatment of colored people in this section of the civilized world" (57). Taking a leaf from his antebellum predecessors in African American autobiography rather than following the lead of his more fashionable black literary contemporaries, Pickens constructed his indictment of southern racial mores on bluntly stated facts from actual first-hand experience. Not content simply to recall anecdotes of oppression and brutality, however, Pickens brought home to his reader the experience of discrimination by personalizing it, by showing how one's very *personality* was always at issue and always at stake in any sort of intercourse with whites under the Jim Crow code.

Through his detailed explanation of the psychological dynamics underlying any and all encounters between the races, through his analysis of the ways in which a word, a gesture, a tone of voice, even the timing of a statement could be freighted with a life-and-death significance that only an insider in the southern racial order could comprehend, Pickens turned the last chapters of *Bursting Bonds* into an unprecedented autobiographical rendition of what Richard Wright would later term "the ethics of living Jim Crow."[16] Instead of the hesitant and confused rebelliousness of the black boy of Wright's autobiographical account, however, the protagonist of *Bursting Bonds* is a black man, mature in his militancy and certain of his cause. The remarkable image Pickens offers of himself in "Arkansas Traveler" sleeping in a forbidden Pullman berth "with the finger of my right hand coiled over the trigger of a deadly weapon" (69) must have been shocking to readers of his day who thought they "knew the Negro" from having read the popular black autobiographies of that time. Alien to so much of the experience recorded in contemporary black autobiography, Pickens's "Arkansas Traveler" episode allies *Bursting Bonds* with the narratives of such dauntless fugitive slave escapees as Henry Bibb, Box Brown, and William and Ellen Craft, while also anticipating the heroic freedom rides narrated in African American autobiographies of the 1960s and 1970s.[17]

The last chapter of *Bursting Bonds* catches Pickens's career on an ascending arc once again as he moves from Wiley University in Texas to Morgan College in Baltimore before finally heading to New York City to become field secretary of the NAACP. Pickens's autobiography may be said to end as it begins, therefore, in an ascent from southern restrictions to northern recognition and opportunities. The implication is that Pickens's ultimate ascent from the South in 1920 was as logical and inevitable as his descent into the South after the fulfillment of his youthful aspirations at Yale in 1904. Having dedicated himself to "fighting ignorance" in the South, Pickens saw no inconsistency in participating in the NAACP's program of "fighting lynching" in the South (60) or in accepting an offer to lead that fight from the headquarters of the association in New York. Leaving the southern scene to return to the North is treated in *Bursting Bonds* not as a reorientation of the author's priorities but as a reconstitution of them for the purpose of direct social action on a larger, national stage. Arriving in New York in 1920 at the outset of what would soon be known as the New Negro decade, Pickens had learned through his cumulative experience of ascent, descent, and ascent once again how to "live in the real" while "fighting for an ideal" (74). This impression of Pickens as a human rights idealist enmeshed in the battlefield of the real identifies the author of *Bursting Bonds* as the kind of New Negro who would realize the longstanding ideals of his people through personal example and broadly based social action.

The importance of *Bursting Bonds* to the history of African American autobiography is not easily summed up. In addition to its pioneering portrayal of the making of a New Negro, the autobiography contributed to a new frankness about life along the color line in the 1920s and a renewed critical perspective on the literary etiquette of black autobiographical expression in the new century. *Bursting Bonds* also forecast the response of several important modern African American writers to what might be called the single-directed traditions of black life-writing left over from the nineteenth century. Interweaving elements from Douglass's classic narrative of ascent in 1845 and Washington's model of the narrative of descent in 1901, *Bursting Bonds* turned what had seemed contradictory in the black autobiographical tradition into something complementary. Ascent and descent are no longer treated as mutually exclusive in Pickens's story—nor would they appear so in subsequent autobiographies of New Negroes like James Weldon Johnson, Langston Hughes, and Zora Neale Hurston. The modern African American autobiographer, beginning with William Pickens, reconceived the archetypal notion of life as a journey so that the idea of one-way linear progression, either from South to North or vice versa, no longer determined the plot or the politics of the genre. The openness of form articulated in the very titles of Johnson's *Along This Way* (1933), Claude McKay's *A Long Way from Home* (1937), Hurston's *Dust Tracks on a Road* (1942), and Hughes's *I Wonder as I Wander* (1956) testifies to the modern black autobiographer's re-envisioning of the pattern and meaning of the life journey for blacks in the new century. The search for new narrative patterns and new ways to explain and authorize their meanings would carry twentieth-century African American autobiography well beyond the work of William Pickens. It is important, nevertheless, to recognize the bonds he burst both for the New Negro of the 1920s and for modern black autobiography in general through his pivotal contributions to African American literary, cultural, and social history.

NOTES

1. Most of the biographical information presented in this introduction is taken from Pickens's autobiography or from Sheldon Avery's *Up from Washington: William Pickens and the Negro Struggle for Equality, 1900–1954* (Newark: University of Delaware Press, 1989).

2. From 1905 to 1906 Pickens wrote five articles for *The Voice of the Negro*, whose principal editor, Jesse Max Barber, endorsed such pioneering militant civil rights organizations as the Niagara Movement, the National Negro American Political League, and the National Negro Conference, the forerunner of the NAACP. Pickens's demand for "equal manhood rights" for African Americans appeared in "Social Equality," *Voice of the Negro* 3 (January 1906), 27. His call for "frank discourse" on the major social questions of the day appeared in "Choose!" *Voice of the Negro* 3 (June 1906), 404.

3. See *Harlem, Mecca of the New Negro*, a special issue of the *Survey Graphic* that Locke edited in March 1925, and his *The New Negro* (New York: Albert

and Charles Boni, 1925), an expansion of the *Survey Graphic* issue published eight months later. For the development of the idea of a New Negro, see Henry Louis Gates, Jr., "The Trope of a New Negro and the Reconstruction of the Image of the Black," *Representations* 24 (Fall 1988), 129–55.

4. Booker T. Washington, N. B. Wood, and Fannie Barrier Williams, *A New Negro for a New Century* (Chicago: American Publishing House, 1900).

5. William Pickens, *The New Negro* (New York: Neale, 1916). The quotation is taken from the dedication to the book. Further quotations will be taken from this edition.

6. *Bursting Bonds* (Boston: Jordan and More, 1923; reprint, Bloomington: Indiana University Press, 1991), p. 50. Further page references to *Bursting Bonds* are from the present edition.

7. Rebecca Chalmers Barton, *Witnesses for Freedom* (New York: Harper and Brothers, 1948), p. 27.

8. Among Washington's protégés who wrote autobiographies in the *Up from Slavery* mold are: William H. Holtzclaw, *The Black Man's Burden* (New York: Neale, 1915); William J. Edwards, *Twenty-Five Years in the Black Belt* (Boston: Cornhill, 1918); Robert Russa Moton, *Finding a Way Out* (Garden City, N.Y.: Doubleday, Page, 1921); and Laurence C. Jones, *Piney Woods and Its Story* (New York: Fleming H. Revell, 1922). Other early twentieth-century black autobiographies that owe much to Washington's precedent are: J. Vance Lewis, *Out of the Ditch: A True Story of an Ex-Slave* (Houston: Rein and Sons, 1910); James D. Corrothers, *In Spite of the Handicap* (New York: George H. Doran, 1916); Henry Hugh Proctor, *Between Black and White* (Boston: Pilgrim, 1925); and Rosa Young, *Light in the Dark Belt* (St. Louis: Concordia, 1929).

9. For a detailed examination of Pickens's relationship to Washington, see Avery, pp. 15–34.

10. Pickens, *The Heir of Slaves* (Boston: Pilgrim Press, 1911). Because *The Heir of Slaves* was reprinted as the first nine chapters of *Bursting Bonds*, any quotations from the earlier autobiography may also be found on the identical page in the original edition of *Bursting Bonds*.

11. Joseph Gould, "*Bursting Bonds*," *Opportunity* 2 (February 1924), 59; and "*Bursting Bonds*," *Nation* 118 (January 16, 1924), 68.

12. Stepto, *From Behind the Veil: A Study of Afro-American Narrative* (Urbana: University of Illinois Press, 1979), p. 167; Gates, "Writing 'Race' and the Difference It Makes," in *'Race,' Writing, and Difference*, ed. Henry Louis Gates, Jr. (Chicago: University of Chicago Press, 1986), p. 9; *Narrative of the Life of Frederick Douglass*, ed. Houston A. Baker, Jr. (New York: Penguin, 1982), p. 78; Austin Steward, *Twenty-Two Years a Slave and Forty Years a Freeman* (1857; rpt. Reading, Mass.: Addison-Wesley, 1969), p. 80; W. E. B. Du Bois, *The Souls of Black Folk* and "The Talented Tenth," in *W. E. B. Du Bois: Writings* (New York: Library of America, 1986), pp. 367, 842.

13. For the ex-slaves' ideas about education, see James D. Anderson, *The Education of Blacks in the South, 1860–1935* (Chapel Hill: University of North Carolina Press, 1988), pp. 4–32. For information on the migrations of black South Carolinians during the 1870s and 1880s see George Brown Tindall, *South Carolina Negroes, 1877–1900* (Columbia: University of South Carolina Press, 1952), pp. 169–85. In *Branches without Roots: Genesis of the Black Working Class*

in the American South, *1862–1882* (New York: Oxford University Press, 1986), Gerald David Jaynes calls Pickens's account of his family's early travails in Arkansas "a classic case of debt bondage" (309).

14. For additional comments on Du Bois's idea of "double-consciousness," which appears in its best known formulation in *The Souls of Black Folk*, see Arnold Rampersad, *The Art and Imagination of W. E. B. Du Bois* (1976; rpt. New York: Schocken, 1990), pp. 74–76; and Thomas C. Holt, "The Political Uses of Alienation: W. E. B. Du Bois on Politics, Race, and Culture, 1903–1940," *American Quarterly* 42 (June 1990), 301–23.

15. For discussion of Pickens's conflict with the administration of Talladega and with the leadership of the American Missionary Association, see Avery, pp. 29–34.

16. See the opening essay in Wright's *Uncle Tom's Children* (New York: Harper and Brothers, 1940).

17. See, for instance, *Narrative of the Life and Adventures of Henry Bibb, an American Slave* (1849); *Narrative of the Life of Henry Box Brown* (1851); *Running a Thousand Miles for Freedom; or, the Escape of William and Ellen Craft from Slavery* (1860); Anne Moody's *Coming of Age in Mississippi* (1968); and Benjamin Mays, *Born to Rebel* (1971).

BURSTING BONDS

FOREWORD

It is a common story; there were more than three million slaves; there are perhaps ten million heirs born of the slaves since 1865. What reason can there be for writing a story which is so common?

One reason is that some want to know the story, and have asked for it. These several requests have been prompted, perhaps, by no expectation of anything wonderful in the story, but by the fact that it is common and can therefore stand as the representative of the class. This last reason is the one that emboldens me to the task. The interests of a class may justify the examination and description of a typical specimen.

I shall therefore regard myself as speaking to friends. I shall not aim to evaluate the thing I say, but I shall simply relate the incidents and leave the worth of them to the judgment of the audience. If I am frank, it is only to be true. Such a story could have no self-glory and little expectation of applause.

PREFACE TO THE
SECOND EDITION

The first edition of "The Heir of Slaves" was published in 1911, when I was still pursuing work as a member of the faculty of Talladega College, Alabama. The readers of the little story have professed much pleasure in it and have made many demands that it be reprinted that others might have it, but a sincere feeling of unworthiness has prevented me from writing it up to date and republishing it before this time (1923).

In the additional chapters I have endeavored to bring up to date, by an outline of the last twelve years, this simple human tale, for the inspiration and benefit of the young and for the satisfaction and pleasure of the more mature.

The hearty reception which the first publication received from all classes of men and women, and especially from the members of other races than my own, was to me a surprise and is still a a thing not quite understood. Most of the readers, when they finished with the first chapter, were tempted to read on to the last page without stopping. Many an eminent and very busy American has said that he picked up the little volume, bought in a sense of charity, with the idea of scanning it a bit before retiring, but that after reading a few pages the reader could not be persuaded to go to rest until the the last word had been read.

To many normal people the plain details of a struggling and earnest life, wherein things are done in hazard and hope, in fear and courage, are more interesting than well calculated fiction wherein difficulties are solved by *deus ex machina*.

WILLIAM PICKENS,
260 West 139th St.,
New York City.

THE HEIR OF SLAVES

ONE

MY PARENTAGE

I was born on the 15th day of January, 1881, according to the recollection of my parents.* There was no record of the sixth child, for the sixth baby is no novelty in a family. But as the historian finds the dates of old battles by the comets and eclipses, so can we approximate this event by an impressive happening: because of the martyrdom of a good President I narrowly escaped the honor of being named *Garfield* Pickens.

With natural and pardonable curiosity people have often asked me about my parentage, and if I knew anything about my ancestry. My immediate parents I know, and have known something of one or two of my grandparents. But about any ancestry more remote than this all that I can know is that it seems natural and logical to conclude by analogy and induction that I probably had some additional forbears. Most of the Negroes in the United States who are as many as thirty years old have no reliable knowledge of ancestry beyond perhaps their grandparents. The family tree is just sprouting or just beginning to put forth shoots. How the causes of this inhered in the system of slavery is well known. There are good and sensible reasons for keeping an ancestral record of certain breeds of horses, but little reason for keeping that of slaves, simply because the worth of a man depends less upon the value and blood of his father than does the price of a horse.

Three-fourths of all the Negroes I have ever seen had other blood. Sometimes it was not visible in their faces: the blackest man may have a mulatto grandmother on his mother's side. And your average brown Negro—if all the different sorts of blood in his veins should get at war with each other, the man would blow up like a stick of dynamite.

My father in color and hair is African although his features are not prominently African, and I knew one of his sisters who was brown. My

---

*William Pickens was the sixth of ten children and the first son born to Jacob and Fannie Pickens, former slaves who gained their freedom after the fall of the Confederacy in 1865.

mother's mother, who lived long in our family and "raised" all of the grandchildren, was a characteristic little African woman, vivacious and longlived, with a small head and keen eyes. She could thread her own needles when she was eighty years of age. She lived for forty years with a broken back, the upper part of her body being carried in a horizontal position, at right angles to her lower limbs, so that she must support her steps with a staff if she walked far. This was one of the results of slavery. Being a high-tempered house-servant in that system she had been beaten and struck across the back with a stick. Even in her old age her temper rose quick, but was volatile, and she was a very dear and most helpful grandmother. My mother's father, whom I never saw, and who perhaps died a slave, was half Cherokee Indian, his father being a Cherokee. I suppose that his other half was Negro, since he was married in slavery to my grandmother.

My mother was an average-sized brown woman, whose features were somewhat modified by her Indian strain and whose hair was black and of a Negro-Indian texture. She was simply famous for the amount of hard work she could do. As a cook she could get a breakfast in the shortest possible time; as a washerwoman she could put out the clothes of a large family by noon. And her work must have been well done, for she could never supply the demand for her services, and she died of overwork at the age of about forty-five. I was the sixth of her ten children.

My birthplace was in Anderson County, South Carolina, near Pendleton, in a rural neighborhood called "over the river," where lies the first dim, flickering memory of the humble estate to which I was born. My parents were farmers of the tenant or day-labor class and were ever on the move from cabin to cabin, with the proverbial unacquisitiveness of the "rolling stone." They were illiterate, but were beginning to learn to read the large-print New Testament sold by the book agents. That part of the state was exceedingly poor, with red hills and antiquated agriculture. From such sections of the old South the immigration agent of the West easily induced many Negroes to cross the Mississippi into debt-slavery. My parents were industrious but improvident, and began early to talk of moving to Arkansas where the soil was fertile and wages high. This was possible only by allowing some Western farmer to pay the fares of the family through his agent, and by signing a contract to work on that farmer's land until the debt was paid according to that farmer's reckoning.

The earliest family moving which I remember was from "over the river" to "Price's place," which makes my memory reach back to my second year. At "Price's" there was our one-room cabin on a small hill facing the larger hill on which stood the "great house" of the landowner. I remember the curiosity of our first clock, an "eight-day" specimen, which my father immediately took to pieces and put together again; and he still boasts that his clock has never been to the repair shop. Here, too, I received the first impression of my personal appearance. I had a large head, for a certain comical minded uncle would play frightened whenever I came near him, and he dubbed that part of my anatomy "a wag'n-body."

After a year or so we moved from "Price's" to "Clark's place," nearer Pendleton. Here I received my first slight acquaintance with the English alphabet, which I learned so readily that my sisters took delight in leading me to school with them, although I must have been at least two years under school age. It was a characteristic Negro schoolhouse built of logs, with one door and one window, the latter having no panes and being closed by a board shutter which swung on leather hinges outward. The house was not larger than a comfortable bedroom and had a "fire-place" opposite the door. The children faced the fireplace, so that the scant light fell through the door upon their books. There were no desks; the seats were long board benches with no backs. The teacher insisted that the students sit in statuesque postures, not moving a limb too often. Persuasion to study and good deportment consisted of a hickory switch, a cone-shaped paper "dunce cap" and a stool on which the offender must stand on one foot for an enormous length of time. Although I had readily learned my elements under sympathetic tutelage at home, about all I remember of this first schooling is the menacing words of the teacher, the movements of that switch and the astonishing balancing acts of the dunce cap wearers. The chief fountain of academic knowledge in such schools was the famous old "blue-back speller." After leaving the nonsense syllables in the beginning of that book, the milestones of attainment were first the page of dissyllables beginning with "baker" and secondly the page of polysyllables containing "compressibility." A person interested in your advancement might ask first had you "got to 'baker' yet," and secondly could you spell "compressibility."

After a year at "Clark's place" we moved to Pendleton, and from that time till I reached the age of eighteen I can count no less than twenty removals of our family.

The motives that carried my mother and father from the country into the little town of Pendleton were more than good; they were sacred. It was a consideration for the future of their children. Having lived nearer town for a year, they learned that the houses, the wages and the schools of the village were superior to those of the country. The country school was poorly housed and still more poorly taught. Its sessions lasted for only a few hot weeks of summer after the "laying by" of the crops, and for a few cold weeks of winter between the last of harvest and the time for clearing the fields. School interests were secondary to farm interests; the raising of children must not interfere with the raising of cotton. The landowner would not tolerate a tenant who put his children to school in the farming seasons. In the town, my mother had cooked and washed, in the country she had been a field hand. A cook has somewhat better opportunities to care for small children; there was a story of how Mother, returning from field work to the railfence where she had laid the baby to sleep, found a great snake crawling over the child. In the country my father worked while another man reckoned.

It always took the whole of what was earned to pay for the scant "rations" that were advanced to the family, and at settlement time there would be a margin of debt to keep the family perennially bound to a virtual owner. A man in town who ran a bar and hotel, and who needed help, offered to pay this margin of debt and bring the whole family to town if Father would be his man of all work and Mother a cook. Wages were small but paid promptly, and there was no binding debt. They went, as one instinctively moves from a greater toward a lesser pain. There was one certain advantage; the children obtained six months instead of six weeks of schooling.

My parents were always faithful members of the Baptist church, and even while my father was hotel man and "bartender," he was superintendent of the Sunday school of his village church. Had he been keeping bar for himself he would have been excommunicated by his brethren. An inevitable, but not inalterable, dual moral system has grown up in the inter-racial life of the South; a Negro may be tolerated by his own race in doing for a white man what would not meet with toleration if done for himself; and a white man may be excused by his own race if he does to a Negro what would be instantaneously condemned if done to a white man.

Twenty odd years ago Pendleton was a characteristic little town of the older South. There was the central public "square" on one side of which stood the "calaboose" and on the opposite side the post office. It was full of politics and whisky, but withal there was extraordinary good feeling between the white and the black race. The employer of my father was the head man of the village, whom the people called "town councilor," a position corresponding to the mayoralty in larger towns. This man was a boon companion of my father, and they ran the town together. Race antagonism seemed not to touch our world. I can remember many things which indicate that race feeling was not nearly as combustible in Pendleton then as it is in most places now. For example, on Christmas Day the black folk used to say that "there is no law for Christmas." And so the young Negro men, in a good-natured spree, would catch the lone policeman, who was always more a joke than a terror, and lock him in the calaboose to stay a part of Christmas Day, while one of the black men with star and club would strut about the town and play officer—an act for laughter then, but which now would summon the militia from the four quarters of almost any state and be heralded the world over as ugly insurrection.

For some reason at this period wages were steadily declining in the older states of the South. In 1887 the wage for doing a day's work or picking a hundred pounds of cotton in the fields was thirty-five or forty cents. The Western immigration agent was busy telling of glorious opportunities beyond the Mississippi, and many minds among black people were being turned in that direction. After several years of village life, and after engaging in various employments, including another year of farming, we moved to Seneca, S.C. Father had been in turn farmer, hotel man, section hand, brakeman and fireman.

In these awakening years, when the mind is supposed to receive so much, I had about two short terms of schooling so poor that in New England it would not be called schooling at all. My mother's constant talk and ambition was to get an opportunity "to school the children." One of the chief causes of the rapid advancement of the Negro race since the Civil War has been the ambition of emancipated black mothers for the education of their children. Many an educated Negro owes his enlightenment to the toil and sweat of a mother.

But "hard times" and the immigration agent were fast persuading my father to risk the future of his family in the malarial swamp-lands of Arkansas.

TWO

TO ARKANSAS

At last an agent representing a planter in the Mississippi River Valley of Arkansas induced my father to sign a contract to move his entire family to that state. In order to appreciate the persuasions which the agent used, the ignorance and superstition of such families would have to be understood. Ignorant people are too quick to believe tales of other places and other times. Our family had a hundred "signs," mostly signs of evil. By the ruddy glow of the fire at nights the children were told of ghosts, of strange cats, dogs, voices and sounds, of the "no-headed man," of graveyards, and the weird history of the ill-famed "three-mile bottom" near the village. The Federal soldiers were described not as common men, but as beings from a super-world; and with the irony of truth Lincoln was pictured as more than mortal.

To such a group reports from the outside world come with a feeling of otherworldliness. The agent said that Arkansas was a tropical country of soft and balmy air, where cocoanuts, oranges, lemons and bananas grew. Ordinary things like corn and cotton, with little cultivation, grew an enormous yield.

On the 15th of January, 1888, the agent made all the arrangements, purchased tickets, and we boarded the train in Seneca, S.C., bound toward Atlanta, Ga. Our route lay through Birmingham and Memphis, and at each change of trains there seemed to be some representative of the scheme to see us properly forwarded, like so much freight billed for we knew not where. It was midwinter, but with all the unquestioning faith and good cheer of our race we expected to land at the other end of our journey in bright sunshine and spring weather.

And a comical-looking lot we must have been. We had no traveling cases, but each one bore some curious burden—sacks of clothes, quilts, bags, bundles and baskets. When we left our home the weather was comparatively mild, but as fate would have it, the nearer we got to Arkansas, the colder it became. In Memphis the snow was deep and the wind biting. The faith and enthusiasm of the party grew less; perhaps the older heads were waking up to a suspicion. The further we got from our South Carolina home, the dearer it seemed, as is true of most things in their first abandonment.

When we reached a small station in Arkansas, like freight again we were met by two double-team wagons of the unknown planter to whom we were consigned. We were hauled many miles through cypress "brakes" and snow and ice sufficiently thick to support the teams. The older people, I suppose, had by this time comprehended the situation, but we children were constantly peering out from under our quilts and coverings, trying to discover a cocoanut or an orange blossom, while the drivers swore at the mules for slipping on the solid ice. Perhaps nothing could equal this disappointment unless it be the chagrin of those ignorant Negroes who have been induced to go to Africa under the persuasion that bread trees grew there right on the brink of molasses ponds, and wild hogs with knives and forks sticking in their backs trotted around ready baked!

When we reached the estate of our consignee, still like freight we were stored away, bags, bundles, boxes and all of us, in a one-room hut to await the breaking of winter and the beginning of field work.

What could we do? The planter had the contract binding us hard and fast. Just what we owed for transportation no one knew; besides we had been furnished with salt meat, meal and molasses for the first weeks of enforced idleness, and we were supplied with a little better food, including sugar, coffee and flour, when field work began. As in the case of any property on which one has a lease, our lessor could lay out more on our maintenance in the seasons when we were bringing returns.

When the first year's settlement came around, and a half hundred bales of cotton had been produced by the family and sold by the planter, Father came home with sad, far-away eyes, having been told that we were deeper in debt than on the day of our arrival. And who could deny it? The white man did all the reckoning. The Negro did all the work. The Negro can be robbed of everything but his humor, and in the bottom lands of Arkansas he has made a rhyme. He says that on settlement day the landowner sits down, takes up his pen and reckons thus:

"A nought's a nought, and a figger's a figger—
All fer de white man—none fer de nigger!"

But we were not long depressed. To keep down debts in the ensuing winter Mother cooked and washed and Father felled trees in the icy "brakes" to make rails and boards. No provisions were drawn from the planter. The old debt remained, of course, and perhaps took advantage of this quiet period to grow usuriously. This low land is malarial, chills and fevers returning like the seasons. Our medicine and physician, too, had to be secured on the feudal plan, the planter paying the bills. Under such a system the physician has the greatest possible temptation to neglect the patient; his pay is sure, and there is no competition. The spring sickness was miserable; we had come from an elevated, healthy country, and our constitutions fell easy prey to the germs of the lowlands.

For the first year the children were kept out of school in hope of getting rid of the debt. Very small children can be used to hoe and pick cotton, and I have seen my older sisters drive a plow. The next year we attended the short midsummer and midwinter sessions of the plantation school. The school was dominated by the interests of the planter; when the children were needed in the fields he simply commanded the school to close. It was an old-fashioned district school, where the spelling classes stood in line with recognized "head" and "foot." Your ability to spell was denoted by your position in the line relative to the "head" and the "foot." When your neighbor toward the head missed a word and you spelled it, you "turned him down" with all others who had missed that word in succession, that is, you took your position above them. If you were absent from a class, when you returned, whatever had been your position in the line, you had to "go foot." I had a sister a year or so older than I, who stood "head" about all of the time, while I stood second; and we used to stay home a day for the exquisite pleasure of going foot and turning the whole class down. This sister had a phenomenal memory when a child.

The second year the whole family plunged into work, and made a bigger and better crop. But at reckoning time history repeated itself; there was still enough debt to continue the slavery. If the debt could not be paid in fat years, there was the constant danger that lean years would come and make it bigger. But there was the contract—and the law; and the law would not hunt the equity, but would enforce the letter of the contract. It was understood that the Negro was unreliable, and the courts must help the poor planters.

There was but one recourse—the way of escape. The attempt must be executed with success, or there might be fine and peonage. On some pretext my father excused himself and went to Little Rock. A few miles out of that city he found a landowner who would advance the fares for the family and rent to us a small farm. This looks at first sight like "jumping from the frying-pan into the fire," but a rented farm with a definite loan is a different proposition from a state of debt-slavery, where the creditor sells all the produce and does all the counting. Moreover, when a condition is about as bad as it can be, there is a tendency in human nature to move on to another bad condition with a sort of desperate venture. Human nature will flee from a known condition that is very bad to an unknown condition that might be worse, in spite of Lord Hamlet's soliloquy. And so one night the young children and some goods were piled into a wagon and the adults went afoot. By morning we were in the town of Augusta, twelve or fifteen miles away, where we caught the first train.

I have one very pleasant recollection of the place from which we had escaped. An aged Negro, a characteristic Uncle Remus,* would come some nights and relate to us quaint animal stories. The antics and cleverness of "Bre'r Rabbit, Bre'r Bar, Bre'r Fox, Sis' Cow and Bre'r Tommy Mud Turtle" did much to enliven the dullness of the hours.

---

*Uncle Remus is the narrator and principal character of Joel Chandler Harris's *Uncle Remus: His Songs and His Sayings* (1880), a famous collection of African American folk tales.

THREE

BEGINNING SCHOOL IN EARNEST

The desperate move to Galloway, in the neighborhood of Little Rock, was by no means an unlucky one. For one whole year, of course, we children were kept out of school to clear up the new debt. The debt was paid. Meanwhile my mother heard that in the city of Little Rock and in the town Argenta, across the river from Little Rock, there were nine months' terms of school. Think of it! Nine months of schooling for the children.

We moved to Argenta in the winter of 1890–91. This move cityward was not prompted, as is usually charged in such cases, by any desire to get away from work, but by the high motives of education and the future. The prospect struck me with so much force that I set to work and learned to write before I could be sent to school. I could not enter at once—work had to be done and means gotten so that we could start in the fall of 1891. All members of the family worked ceaselessly, about the homes in the city and on the farms near the city. While running errands and making fires at a certain hotel I saw and recognized the face of a quack doctor, a man with long hair, who had once come through the bottom lands from which we had escaped and had frightened my mother out of all her ready cash for his cure-all medicines by telling her that I had consumption. Mentioning the incident to him, "Are you the man?" asked I, with boyish frankness. And he, with quack-doctor frankness, replied, "That depends, my boy, upon whether the medicine helped or hurt you, and upon whether you would like to buy some more."

The Argenta schools opened in September. We could not attend regularly in the weeks that preceded Christmas, for we were at work picking cotton in the neighboring fields. It took the energies of the whole family to get a start. My attendance before Christmas was for only a few scattering days. After Christmas, however, I started in school not to miss another day during that school year—not to miss another day for the next seven years' school years—and indeed not to miss another unnecessary day until I had finished at Yale in 1904.

This was my real start in school, and I was now nearly eleven years old. As a peaceful country boy I was at first imposed upon, but one fine day I laid aside my unwarlike habits and became sufficiently belligerent to win the respect of a certain class of my fellows. I had to fight my way on the playground as well as in the classroom, and at the same time I had to render my accounts and make my peace with the stern government of a teacher who was a fine instructor and a severe disciplinarian—just the proper governor for such a rebellious little state as a city public school. I remember how at the end of that school year he called me out, with his brows lowering as if a storm was going to break, and sternly commanded me to take my seat on the bench in front of his desk—the well-known judgment seat where many a little sinner had been called to a sure, even if a reluctant, repentance. I began mentally to review my day's record in order to anticipate the accusation, when he with the same sternness of voice began to pronounce, "This boy"—then hesitating and transfixing me with his terrible eye—"entered school three months late, started behind everybody else, and now he's the leader of his class!"

This teacher's name was J. S. Pleasant, and although he was very strict, the name is not at all inapplicable to his general character. He was my teacher for the following four years. Very often when the teacher had passed a question or a problem around to all the rest of the class and they had failed to answer or to solve it, he would say, "Well, 'Always Ready' will take it"—which was a nickname he sometimes applied to me.

In a personal history I might be expected to tell about my school career and record. In mathematics I never received less than 100 per cent. as a daily average, and only once did I make less than 100 per cent. on an examination in that subject. I state this fact because so many men and women of the white race have asked me particularly how I fared in the subject of mathematics.

I committed my lessons to memory. The lessons in physiology and history I learned verbatim every day, so that I could repeat them, just as they were written, with as much ease as I can say the Lord's Prayer. When I reached the high school we had a large book known as "Barnes's

General History." The lessons were from five to ten pages, and I had acquired the ability to commit them by reading them three times over. This I did every day. The history teacher at the end of the year, after having me stand and recite the last lesson verbatim, said, "I never believed that he would go through this whole book in that way." For the last few minutes of each recitation during the year she had asked me to rise and go through the whole lesson, as in declamation. She would then question me, evidently to see if I knew the *parts* as well as the *whole*. Any question in the lesson would be answered; I had not learned by sound merely.

I was deeply in love with school and study. Very often I reached the schoolhouse before the janitor arrived. From the nickels and dimes which I received for errands and small jobs I would save sufficient money to buy my books. When I was attending the grammar school my mother endeavored one day to keep me at home to draw water for the washing. She never tried it again—I cried and pleaded as if my heart would burst. The prospect of missing my classes for a day seemed to me absolutely unbearable. It seemed that it would tear down all that I had builded. My mother seized a switch to chastize me, but when she listened to my words and looked into my face she saw that it was not rebellion, and with a rather satisfied laugh she said that I might go, if I was that "crazy" about school. I can see now that she was rather proud of the event, for never again did she make any arrangement that would keep me out of school for a day. The whole family came to regard my attendance at school as a foregone conclusion. The children called me "old man," because I would not play until after I had learned my lessons. These were almost invariably learned before sundown. At the end of that very year I received from the teacher a prize for being "never absent, never tardy." It was a book entitled "Our Manners and Social Customs," and it was the first book outside of a school text that I had ever read.

The opportunity which a mother's pride created for my schooling during her life could not continue after her death. She died of overwork and consequent broken health. She had been determined to keep her children in school and had worked from early morning till late at night to that end. We seldom waked early enough to catch a glimpse of her, and before her return at night sleep had weighed down the eyelids of the younger children.

I had just entered upon my fourth year in the city school when my mother died in October. Imagine, if you can, the sorrow and confusion, amounting almost to dismay, that filled the heart and mind of a boy of thirteen, who was ambitious and who knew that his mother was the mainstay of his education and his future—a boy who loved school as dearly as any other boy ever loved a gun or a motor-cycle. I knew what my mother had meant to the family and that without her it would be impossible for my father to keep all the children in school. It was her love and ambition, I knew, that had given me the high privilege of study, and without her I could not be certain of my daily bread for the school year on which we had just entered.

But the ways of Providence are inscrutable, and this confusion and predicament thrust upon me a blessing. I secured a place to earn my board by rising at four o'clock in the morning and also working after school hours until seven o'clock in the evening—and I got my lessons just as well, or better than ever before. Out of misfortune and a hard situation I had to pluck independence.

In this temporary confusion one thought was of more permanent help to me than all other things. Mother had taught us to believe in God, and I reasoned that God would not cause such a good mother to begin such a good work and then remove that mother without intending that in some other way that work was to go on. The thought led me on and on to a greater and greater faith in my opportunities.

FOUR

A SKIFF-FERRY SCHOOL BOY

In the following year I became a ferryman on the Arkansas River to support myself during the last year of the grammar school. The grammar school at that time completed the ninth year, the high school adding three years more.

The town of Argenta, which for a brief space bore the appellation of North Little Rock, is situated, as the latter name implies, on the left bank of the Arkansas River opposite the City of Little Rock. In the early '90's Argenta was famed as one of the worst places in the United States; debauchery, blood and murder were no uncommon spectacles. The incoming traveler shrugged his shoulders when he heard the name "Argenta."

At that time there were only two railroad bridges, adapted also for foot and wagon passage; and all passers had to pay toll, the foot fare per capita being five cents. This condition gave rise to another industry, carried on chiefly by Negro men, that of a "skiff ferry." These small boats in which the boatman uses two oars and sits with his back towards the fore, were used to row passengers over the Arkansas to and from Argenta to the foot of Main Street in Little Rock. The fare had been five cents, but under the stress of competition it had become by this time five cents for the round trip. There were about a dozen skiffmen earning each from two to three dollars a day. I quickly mastered all this ferry-craft, sometimes rowing a boat myself and sometimes working as a second oarsman, assisting one of the men. My average wage was about forty cents a day. When I rowed a boat alone I received more; when I rowed as an assistant my pay was at the mercy of the principal, and he paid me according to his earnings or his fancy. I was soon as good an oarsman as any man I worked with, but I was only a school boy, fourteen years of age, and no one would think of paying me a man's wages even for a man's work. But the pittance was saving me my education and my future; and boy although I was, I looked at the present circumstance in the light of the future, and never thought that the condition was too hard, but only the high price of a valuable possession.

This river work also profited me physically; the use of two oars is conducive to symmetry of body, and there is no danger of the one-sided development which Ben-Hur dreaded from the one-oar method of the Roman galley.* There had been some family doubts about the soundness of my constitution, after the hard wear in the bottom lands of Arkansas, but this ferry work remade my shoulders and chest and lungs. During the school year I could row on Saturdays, and could get a boat by myself on Sundays and work until Sunday school time and afterwards.

I worked again on the ferry in the summer of 1896, and any ferryman was glad to have my services, as I was an able oarsman and also a hustler in securing passengers.

During the summer of 1896 a new problem was before me for solution in reference to my education. I had entered the Argenta school five years before, knowing nothing save to read and spell simple words and to write in my self-taught style. I had not missed a day or an hour of school since that first year, and I had led all of my classes all of the time. The grammar school course was now completed and to stop seemed a calamity. There was no high school in the district and no accessible private school; besides, I could not pay for private instruction. There was a High School in Little Rock to which students from our side of the river could not go except by special permission of the school authorities, and only then by paying two dollars and fifty cents per month. I could not have much hope of getting into this school, but against the bare possibility I saved my earnings on the ferry, bought none of the things which would please a boy of fifteen years, and came to the end of the summer with about forty dollars in a savings bank, practically every cent that I had earned.

There was one fortunate circumstance: the principal of the Argenta school was a boarder in the home of the principal of the Little Rock High School and had constantly praised me as a student. Some days before the opening of school I was called to the home of the High School principal to take the entrance examinations. I have heard him

---

*Judah Ben-Hur, hero of Lew Wallace's bestselling novel *Ben Hur* (1880).

say since that in each of the subjects of arithmetic, grammar, United States history and spelling I was marked 100 per cent., and that especially in the subject of arithmetic he had looked up "catch" problems to test the value of my former principal's praises. However that may be, when I went to register at the offices of the Board of Education, I was not too minutely questioned as to the "residence of parents," etc., the superintendent taking no seeming notice of the fact that I was from over the river. And when I reached the secretary's desk in the line of applicants and received my certificate of entrance to the High School of Little Rock, what a critical moment was passed, what a vista was opened for me! Three more years of schooling were assured. I could work on the ferry in summer and at week-ends to buy necessary books and clothing. I plunged into that High School work with a zest such as I have seldom experienced since. My never-absent, never-tardy record was maintained, and indeed during the three High School years only once was I absent, and then because of an illness that took me for a day in the spring of my last year.

When I entered the High School the class had had a beginners' algebra for one year, and were now taking up the more advanced book. I had never studied that subject, but at the end of the first month or so I was ranked first in that study. These High School classmates set out for my scalp, for my conquest and undoing. They seemed to presume, what men usually presume under similar circumstances, that the new comer is unduly ambitious, that he is simply "showing off" because he is new, and that the pace which he has set will not and cannot last. They attacked me on every side; they picked every possible flaw in my work and recitations, and in their zeal they sometimes found impossible flaws. They laughed; they ridiculed; they studied; they worked valiantly. I kept on. They only stimulated me; they filled me with a most exhilarating feeling for my work. They did for my education what no teacher in the world could have done; they made me study and learn what I had previously supposed I knew. They combined; they attacked first in one subject, then in another. They succored each other clandestinely. But each month and term told for me a better and better story. And before the end of my High School course I had reached that uninteresting point in the career of a winner where his rivals give up and concede him victories which he does not win, and the teachers had often to upbraid my classmates for letting errors go by unchallenged simply because I had made them. But in conquering their admiration

I did not lose their love. I had played fair, and they were not slow to appreciate the fact.

And how did I support myself meanwhile? My father gave me what assistance he could afford; wages were poor and there were younger children. And his groceryman was continually telling him that if he were in father's place he would not allow an able-bodied boy to go to school while he himself worked.

And other men? Well, other men praised me; they did not assist me. And perhaps it is better that human nature is constituted so; men will praise a struggler when they have no thought of helping him. Help is very often a doubtful blessing, and sometimes praise is too, and this reflection is a convenient solace to those who would not help. If every person who named me "smart" should have been required by law to give me a nickel I should have had at least no financial troubles.

During my first year in the High School I continued to work on the ferry. But when summer came again, my success was threatened by a new danger; the public-spirited citizens of Little Rock were building a "free bridge" across the Arkansas River from the foot of Main Street, and this bridge was to be opened on the Fourth of July. The famous old ferry that had existed from the foundation of the city was then to die. The passing of the old ferry seemed the passing of a friend. I had usually carried a book on my oarsman's seat so that I could read or study while waiting for passengers; and as I rowed to and fro I had conjugated Latin verbs to the stroke of the oars.

In the face of a free bridge how was I to prepare for the Middle Year of the High School and pursue it during the term?

FIVE

THE STAVE FACTORY AND THE SAWMILL LUMBER YARD

There was a "stave factory" and cooper shop in Argenta for the manufacture of barrels and kegs, and one thing that comes into the process of making the barrel heads is to stack the green boards, when they are first sawed from the blocks, and to construct the stack so that air circulation will dry them. They were piled in polygonal hollow squares by first laying a polygon of the pieces of "headin' " on the ground and then continuing round and round as the stack grew higher, up to fifty or more feet, or as high as the one on the ground who was "pitchin' headin'," could shoot the short boards up through the air to the one on the stack who was "layin' headin'."

Here I secured a position luckily, and I had an experience at "layin' headin' " which I shall never forget, and which forms as integral a part of my mental and moral training as any other thing I ever did or any book I ever studied. I was earning "six bits" or seventy-five cents a day, more money than I had ever received steadily before in my life. When an older person did the work which I was doing he received usually one dollar a day. But I was a boy and schoolboy at that, and this fact, though otherwise and elsewhere exemplary, lowers one's price in a "stave factory." The superintendent would not pay a schoolboy one dollar a day, and I doubt whether he would have hired me at all if he had not supposed that like almost all others I would never return to school after finding a position that paid four dollars and fifty cents a week, for I remember how he swore when I quit at the end of the summer, calling me a young fool for throwing away the opportunity of certain employment for the doubtful blessings of "schooling." And the fact of my receiving a lower wage brought me into disfavor with some of the men who worked about the factory, especially with the man who "pitched headin' " to me.

This man was at one and the same time, about as merry and human and as cruel and brutal a fellow as my brain has ever been able to imagine. And nothing that I shall record here has the least feeling of resentment toward his memory, for I regard him as one of my appointed teachers who, whether he willed it or not, gave me (somewhat against my will, too) a most valuable mental and moral discipline. If I should meet him today, I would shake his hand heartily as one of my bene-factors, albeit he tried for weeks and weeks to knock my brains out with pieces of green barrel heading. Usually if a man tries constantly to hurt you and you constantly prevent him, he helps you, advances you in the world, the damages which nature assesses in your favor for the unjust attacks upon your life and character. This man was hard as iron in face and heart; stout as an ox in frame; tireless as a machine in action. His wickedness was simple, straightforward; the only good phase of his character was his honest disclaimer of all goodness. He could preach mock sermons as he worked, almost word for word and sound for sound imitations of some of the noisier preachers of the town. He would sing church songs, plantation songs, ribald songs, keeping time to the rhythm of his iron muscles as he sent the pieces of heading shooting into the air. When his jokes were not coarse they were of a good wit and lightened the burdens of all who worked near him.

This man determined to stop me from working at that factory by catching me off my guard and dealing me a terrible blow with a piece of that heading under the excuse of pitching it in the regular way. I felt his determination from the very first by that defensive telepathy with which Nature endues the mind of hunted animals and especially of a hunted man. I was on my guard. I was equally determined to defeat him without ever saying a word to indicate that I suspected him. I must be alert, with my attention fixed from seven o'clock in the morning till noon, and in the afternoon from one o'clock till six. For a long time he tried to wear me out by keeping the pieces of heading flying at me in such rapid succession that there was not a moment even to look aside. But that plan could not succeed, for my work was lighter than his and my nerve and muscles were good. His determination grew with his defeat. He next tried the scheme of pitching with gentle regularity for long periods of time, then suddenly sending up two or more pieces in rapid succession, the last coming with a force to fell an ox. But I was on my guard and both pieces would sometimes be deftly caught to show my skill and vex the tyrant; or when a particularly

murderous shot was fired I might incline my body and let it pass harmlessly by and fall to the ground many yards beyond the stack. At such
times he would swear roughly and say that he was not to waste his time
pitching heading upon the ground. I would make some reasonable remark, trying never to show, or rather determined never to acknowledge
that I understood his aim. He knew well that I understood. I have
known him to walk away out of sight and slip back from another direction, without my notice, as he thought, and send a piece of heavy
heading hissing through the air. It was always either caught or allowed
to pass harmlessly by. I have known him to purchase a water-melon
from a passing wagon, burst it and apparently sit down to eat it, when
suddenly, towards the top of the stack on which I stood, several pieces
of heading would be traveling in swift and dangerous succession. Not
once did he catch me off my guard. I overheard him remark to another
man that I was as hard to hit as a squirrel.

Ill success never discouraged him; he was as persevering as the devil.
All summer he kept up his attack; all summer I kept up my defense.
If I experienced any feeling like hatred in the beginning, it was very
soon all lost, and I came to look upon the daily action as a *contest* in
which it was "up to me" to win.

In September, I returned to school and the superintendent swore.
My friend of the summer's battle dealt gently with me in the last week
or so; perhaps with honest intentions, but without inducing me to take
down my defenses. I came away with no scar or mark, save the blackness
of my palms, which the green-oak sap had rendered blacker than the
backs of my hands.

During the following school season I helped myself by doing odd jobs
on Saturdays and by running errands and cutting wood out of school
hours. I learned my lessons while going errands or chopping wood.
Many people can remember seeing me go along the public streets with
a book open before my face. On a long errand I might commit a whole
history lesson to memory. When I was cutting wood I opened my book
and propped it against a piece of wood at a convenient distance, with
a chip holding the leaves apart, and studied by glances as I swung the
ax.

Later in the year I found another means of help. My father was
fireman for a sawmill and secured for me the privilege of employing
some of my Saturdays on the lumber yards. I was later given the position
also of "Sunday watchman" for these mill-yards. This kept me absolutely

away from Sunday school and away from the day services of the church, but such things I always accepted as temporary means to an end. All day Sunday I camped alone but with my books. If it was cold I made a fire in the mill office and read, and wrote poems, sometimes satires on the members of some class of the High School with which my class was for the moment at war. If the weather was mild I studied or read out on the lumber piles. I early acquired the habit of getting weeks and sometimes months ahead of my class in the text-books. If a subject was to last all the year, I usually finished it in March. When I again went over the work with the class I enjoyed the peculiar profit which comes from review.

During the summer of 1898, preparatory to my senior year in the High School, I worked as janitor in Keys's Business College for white boys. I used to go early to my work in order to study the various books, practice on the typewriting machines and learn the use of certain athletic tools. Under such circumstances the presumption always lies that the janitor is ignorant; but when the boys found out that I could do their lessons for them and out-do their feats on the punching bag and the horizontal bar, some of them grew cold and distant and others enjoyed the exhibitions of my intelligence much as one might enjoy the cleverness of a Simian in the Bronx Park.

My senior year went on as the others had gone. A reporter for one of the daily papers visited the school that year and found us reading Vergil's "Æneid." The teacher had me scan or read metrically, and the next day there appeared in that newspaper a statement that the reporter found a Negro boy that possessed the language of the Romans although he had the color of Erebus.* In that same year also a prominent lawyer who held the office, I think, of attorney-general of the state visited the school and saw and heard some performances in mathematics and Latin, and kindly invited me down to his office to help him convince his law partner that a Negro could learn Latin. I went on my missionary journey. After quite an extended hearing from various parts of Cicero and Vergil and a theoretical discussion between the two lawyers about the relative value of "rote-learning," the partner in question acknowledged that he was convinced—always addressing the other lawyer, and never addressing or noticing me any more than one would address the

---

*In Greek myth, Erebus is the name for primeval darkness.

machine whose qualities and capacities were the subject of discussion. He finally said that I might profit somewhat by a college education— and by his partner I was thanked and dismissed. It reminds me of certain great educational gatherings to discuss the education of the Negro, where the Negro is conspicuous by his enforced absence.

In June of 1899 I was graduated as the valedictorian of my class. This valedictory was the first original address I had ever made; it was forty minutes long. And although that speech was the "apple of mine eye" then, when I think of it now it seems strange to me that I should ever have been allowed to pour forth in that park such a tropical effusion in the presence of the school board and the assembled multitude.

This first graduation, where most men stop, filled me with the greatest desire I have ever experienced for further education. How that mountain of difficulty was climbed shall be related now. The summer immediately following my High School graduation wrote into the story of my life another of those delicious chapters of hard and profitable experience to which I turn and read whenever I am tempted by discouragement.

SIX

"YOU CAN HAVE HOPE"

This was a truly critical time in my career. I knew that I was not even half educated. I desired to go to college—but how? I thought I should have to work for several years and save the money. But I knew that it is not well to interrupt one's education; a thing that is well started goes more easily if it is not allowed to stop. But necessity is necessity, and I had become used to stooping to conquer before her iron rod. So I took the state teacher's examination and secured a "first grade" license. I could have earned forty or fifty dollars a month at teaching.

I knew that most young men of my acquaintance when they could earn fifty dollars a month felt no further need of school. But I did not fear that such a feeling would ever take possession of me. I had come to have a stout faith; whatever difficulty I met, I believed that in some way I could get over it. If faith ever becomes dangerous, mine had perhaps reached that dangerous point where I felt too literally sure that "I cannot fail if I try." I had kept at school for the eight years past because I felt sure that I could do so. I had never failed to solve a problem in all of my lessons, and I had never tackled one with the feeling that I should fail. Always starting out penniless and ever with some new difficulty in my path, I had earned pennies and pushed my way through school from year to year since my mother died. I had overcome many difficulties, never doubting that I should overcome.

At this time I picked up a dusty, worn book that had come into our family by some accident and had lain unopened for years, I read in it a story which filled me with the feeling that mere empty "faith" that is unaccompanied by constant and *faithful* "works" is a comical and a ludicrous phantom. The story ran that a British scholar named More believed in the doctrine of transubstantiation, that *if one believes it*, the bread of the sacrament becomes the actual body and the wine the actual blood of Christ. Erasmus did not believe that doctrine, and so journeyed to England to have a friendly discussion with More.* They met at table without being introduced, neither knowing who the other was. In that day scholars of different nationalities made Latin their international language. A discussion began on the topic of transubstantiation. More, not knowing with whom he was arguing, stood up for the faith; Erasmus, not knowing whom he was opposing, said that he did not believe that faith could transubstantiate matter. Erasmus discovered his opponent through his argument and cried out: "Aut tu Morus es, aut nullus!" (Either you are More, or nobody.) And More with ready wit replied: "Aut tu es Erasmus, aut diabolus!" (Either you are Erasmus or the devil.) Then More claimed that the doctrine was true for those who *believed* it, and that the act of faith made the fact. And Erasmus, outdone in argument, decided not to be outdone in demonstration, and when he was returning to the continent, he asked More to lend him his horse, saying simply that More would surely get his horse back. But when he reached his home in Europe, instead of sending back the horse, he sent to More the two following stanzas:

> "Quod mihi dixisti
> De corpore Christi:
>   'Crede quod edas et edis'—
> Sic tibi rescribo
> De tuo palfrido:
>   Crede quod habeas et habes."

And although I have seen neither the book nor the story since, I remember that I made the following mental rendition of those stanzas into English:

> "What you to me have said
> About the sacred bread:
>   'Believe it's Christ's body and it's that'—
> So I write back to you
> About your palfrey too:
>   Believe that you have it and you hav't."

---

*Sir Thomas More (c. 1477–1535), a leading English humanist and lord chancellor under King Henry VIII, and Desiderius Erasmus (c. 1467–1536), the famed Dutch humanist who wrote his *Praise of Folly* at the suggestion of More, were friends and correspondents during the early sixteenth century.

The story impressed me: how was a fellow to get his horse or win his spurs through mere faith without acts? I inquired of my friends if it were not possible for one to work his way in college. The pastor of the First Congregational Church of Little Rock, a graduate of Talladega College in Alabama,* offered to write an intercessory letter to that institution if I could permit him to say how much I should be able to pay toward my college expenses in cash—and that was the "rub." But I told him to write for conditions and that I would set to work to earn the required cash. He gave me the address of the president of the school and I also wrote a frank letter. It was now July and I could not wait for a reply; I must set to work in the hope of earning an acceptable amount of cash. I entered again upon one of those life experiences which are hard enough in their passage, but which in their recollection verify the truth of Vergil's line, that "perchance some day it will be pleasant to remember even these things."

The new railroad, then popularly known as the "Choctaw," was being built through the wilderness of Arkansas, through sections where neither railroads nor other enginery of civilization had ever gone before. My father was at work on the line forty miles up the Arkansas River, in a tangled jungle only accessible to river boats. Concrete bridges were being built over the streams and gorges, and cuts were being blasted through the hills. It was rough work that only the hardiest men could stand. There is always a chance to secure a position in such work; it is so hard that vacancies are constantly occurring, but the summer was wearing away and I must hurry. I wrote my father that I was coming, and did not wait for his reply, for I knew he would think it impossible for me to do the work.

After journeying a day and a night, working my way on a river steamer among the "roustabouts," I reached the frontier-like scene of a railroad camp. The bulk of the laborers and camp-followers were of the scum of humanity, white and black; there were rough, coarse men and undesirable women. My father tried to act the presumption that I had come to visit him; he studiedly said nothing to me to imply that he had any idea of my attempting that work. I coolly told him of my prospects for going to college, and that I had come to work. I shall

---

*Talladega College in Talladega, Alabama, was established in 1867 by the Congregationalist American Missionary Association as an institution of higher learning for blacks.

never forget the wistful, anxious, half-sad look of his eyes as I took up
my spade and wheelbarrow and went "on the grade" among the men.
There were shoveling and wheeling of dirt and crushed stone. Concrete
mixing machines were not then in use, and the mixing had to be done
by the men with shovels—the heaviest, hardest work imaginable. On
my first day at concrete-mixing the men laughed and swore that I could
not last till noon, but would "white-eye." That term was applied to
the actions of the sufferer because his eyeballs rolled in a peculiar
manner, showing the white, when he became overheated and fell upon
the ground. I did last till noon; and then the foreman, a stocky German
of the coarsest possible nature, who had kept a half amused eye on me
all the morning, expecting to have some fun when I should "white-
eye," was so touched by the determination with which I stuck till noon
that he gave me lighter work. At nights I had only vitality enough left
to bathe in the green waters of the bayou and lie down to rest in my
tent. On Sundays I read two borrowed books, one of them being "Uncle
Tom's Cabin." Most of the men gambled all day Sundays and caroused
till late at night. My better habits soon gave me superior strength and
endurance and I could tire the toughest rival. This seemed wonderful
to the men. They seemed to think that I was a strange fellow. They
did not reckon on the habits of life.

For about a month I had received no word from the president of
Talladega College as to whether my application could be accepted,
when one day there came in the steamboat mail a card, bearing the
Ohio postmark and signed "G. W. Andrews":

"Your frank and interesting letter has been received. I cannot say
definitely now, but write to say you can have hope."

"*You can have hope.*" That was after all a great message at the right
time and place. It seemed to anticipate a more definite reply. I worked
all summer on that card of "hope." Not another word ever came. In
the multitude of the president's duties, and perhaps of similar appli-
cations, my case had doubtless slipped from his memory and notes. But
I hoped and worked, and worked and hoped. September came and wore
away towards October. No word. But there was "hope." I had heard
that Talladega College was to open on the first Tuesday of October.

Meanwhile my evident intelligence had won for me a little better
position from the good-natured, coarse-spoken German, and for my
last month I was put to assist the cook and keeper of the commissary
boat. My father had returned to the city to engage in other work. I

did not tell the foreman that I was going to quit and go to school. I knew better: most of my pay was still due and it would have been all kept and I myself kept for a period. There was no law in that wilderness but the law of the jungle. I had seen the foreman chasing white men with a revolver, as one might chase rabbits.

On the Saturday before the first Tuesday in October I drew all my pay and got excused to go to the city, as the men sometimes did. The steamer was not in, so I had to cross the river and walk fifteen or twenty miles to the nearest railroad station. I left at daylight and caught the train at noon.

It was an uncivilized world from which I had escaped, the only appearance of civilization being from its uglier phase, leased convicts with their "coon-tail" stripes on a farm in a lone valley half a dozen miles from the railroad camps. As one journeyed through the woods he would occasionally come upon a path which would lead to the hut of poor white people; they usually had no floor or chairs and slept on rude "bunks" or on quilts upon the bare ground. It has always appealed more powerfully to my sympathies to behold poor, degraded white people than to behold the same class of my own race. I suppose it is because the degraded white man is such a contrast to the opportunities and attainments of his race, so that his position seems to be a real *de*gradation, and it is a less sad spectacle to see a man simply *down* than to see a man *downed*.

On Sunday I went to see the Congregational preacher, told him of the card of "hope," and that I had had no further word. He concluded that the president had overlooked me, but said that he had heard that if a worthy student could deposit thirty or forty dollars with the treasurer he might be given sufficient work to meet the rest of his bills for the year. Examining my accounts I found that I had to my credit about fifty dollars; my fare from Little Rock, Ark., to Talladega, Ala., would be about fifteen dollars; so that I could spend five dollars for some necessary articles and go with the minimum of thirty dollars.

I went. I was actuated by faith and the "hope." It was something of a venture for a boy of eighteen, who had never before left the neighborhood of home and home-folk. But how was one to get his horse unless to faith he should add deeds?

SEVEN

A CHRISTIAN MISSIONARY COLLEGE

I reached Talladega at night and went early the next morning to the home of the college president, to try my fate again as I had tried it three years before with the high school authorities in Little Rock. He had forgotten me, but remembered when I mentioned the "card of hope." With the coolness and slowness of one who has prepared to look fate in the face I said: "Not hearing any more from you I decided to come and see. And"—drawing something slowly from my pocket— "and I have here *three ten* dollar bills." I noticed the change in the good man's countenance between the words *three* and *ten*; too often had he faced the difficulty of finding a way for apparently worthy students who brought less than a tenth part of their year's expenses. When he learned that I had come five hundred miles on faith, the smile that lit his countenance was auspicious. My star of "hope" had not misled me. He said that he would give the thirty dollars to the treasurer, and asked if I could hitch a horse, milk a cow and work a garden. I replied that I could learn to do any kind of work.

My faith and adventure evidently made a great impression on this man. In his chapel talk that morning, without calling names or making indications, he told a story to the assembled students, how a young man had written from a distant state; how the correspondence had been lost and forgotten; how the fellow had based his hope on a rather indefinite proposition, had worked hard all summer to earn a few dollars, had come many miles. He described the coolness with which this young man had faced him and his own shifting emotions between the words "three" and "ten."

I had not seen a school test all summer, and in my entrance examinations I learned what an excellent preparation it is *not to prepare* for an examination, but to learn each daily lesson and then take a period of rest and not of cramming just before the test. And for the remainder of my school life I prepared for the examination of tomorrow by retiring at eight or nine o'clock the night before.

First the Latin teacher started in to test me in Cicero, which I read so easily that he closed it and opened Vergil's "Æneid," asking me to scan and read. I announced that I could read the first six books, and he turned from book to book, forwards and backwards, but I always "scanned and read." I was then passed on to the teacher of mathematics. Many white people have an honest opinion that the Negro mind is characteristically unmathematical. The teacher asked me to draw the figure and demonstrate the proposition that the sum of three angles of a triangle is equal to two right angles. He added that he would go about some desk work and that I might call his attention when I was ready. As a good-natured resentment to this last statement I called his attention at once, drawing the figure "free-hand" as I did so, and announced that I was "ready." It is a simple and easy proposition, and it was so clearly demonstrated that this teacher, who was the college dean, gave me no further examinations and enrolled me in the sophomore class. So I never was a *freshman.*

I noticed that I was not put to milking cows and hitching teams, willing as I was, but was given work in the college library. In the first of January came the annual week "of prayer," and I joined the little Congregational church which is fostered in connection with the college. I was just about nineteen years old. Why had I not become a church member before this time? That is a thing worth explaining in the interest of the younger generation of Negroes. I believed in God and the church, and had always been a most faithful worshiper, but I could not dream dreams and see visions. Without dreams and visions no one was allowed to join the average Negro church of the past. The cause that produced many of the Negro songs was the fact that the candidate was required to bring and sing a "new song" to prove that he was really converted by God, for the doctrine was that "the devil can convert you, but he can't give you a new song." Rather suggestive, this idea of the unpoeticalness of the devil. It would amuse more than it would instruct for me to relate some of the ridiculous stories which I have heard accepted in church as convert's "experiences." At last I had found a church which did not require that I visit hell, like Dante, in a dream, to be chased by the hounds of the devil and make a narrow, hair-raising escape. And I have been a member of this church since my first college year.

Talladega College is a typical monument of unselfishness. There is nothing in the annals of human history that outrivals the unselfishness that founded and has maintained these institutions for half a century. When the institution was founded in 1867 practically the whole Negro population was illiterate and penniless. It is on record that many workers gave their services absolutely free. The sentiment of the South was naturally opposed to Negro education, especially at the hands of its late enemies. The early workers had to face something more than mere social ostracism: the Ku Klux Klan did not stop with that barbarity of civilization, but often adopted real barbarities, terrifying, banishing, whipping and killing. It is interesting to note what an *evolutionary* influence a school like Talladega has on the sentiment of its neighborhood; white people of the town are now among its chief defenders whenever danger is threatened, and are among its best donors when a new building is to be erected.

And oh, the devolvements of Father Time! The building which has been the main educational hall of the institution for forty years, was erected by slave labor in 1852–53 as a college for white boys. One of the slaves who toiled at the work has since had his many children and grandchildren educated in it.

In my first winter at Talladega I won the college oratorical contest and several other literary prizes. This suggested to the president and faculty the idea of sending me to the North in the following summer with a party of four other students and a teacher on a campaign in the financial interest of the college. The teacher, who has since become President Metcalf, presented the work, the aims and the needs of the institution, the quartet of boys sang and I delivered an address which I prepared especially for the campaign. That speech and that campaign proved to be the doorway of my future, as will appear.

It was in the summer of 1900, and it was my first time north of the Ohio and the Potomac. We went northward in the month of June through Tennessee and Kentucky into Ohio, thence eastward, visiting Niagara and the summer haunts of the rich in the Adirondacks and concluding our campaign in the New England States in September.

It was Commencement time when we reached Oberlin, and the class of 1875 was celebrating its twenty-fifth anniversary. Professor Scarborough of Wilberforce University,* the Negro scholar who is a member of this class, was present at an impromptu parlor entertainment by the five boys of our party, and he so much liked a recitation which I combined from Spartacus** to the Gladiators and The Christian Gladiator that when we parted he gave me in the act of handshaking a silver half dollar. I noticed what he did not notice, that the coin bore the date of "1875," the year of his class—and I have it now, black with age and nonuse in my purse.

At Akron, O., an event happened on which hangs a chain of circumstances; the people requested that my speech be printed in pamphlets so that copies could be purchased. Copies were sent to Dr. G. W. Andrews, the head of Talladega College, the author of my "card of hope." He marked a copy and sent it to Dr. A. F. Beard, the senior secretary of the American Missionary Association.

This trip impressed me with the unselfish spirit of the Christian people of the North—and also showed me that the good people of the North had a very inadequate idea of the real capacity of the American Negro. When we visited the summer camp of Mr. Harrison, ex-president of the United States, members of his party expressed frank surprise that a party of Negro college students could sing and speak and deport themselves so well—and I myself was scrutinized with a most uncomforting curiosity.

Our little campaign paid expenses and brought back a thousand dollars for the college—a small sum of money but a big experience. Moreover I had seen Yale, had actually looked upon its elms, its ivies and its outer walls. From that day the audacious idea began to take me that I must push my educational battles into its gates.

---

*William S. Scarborough (1852–1926) taught classics and published extensively in the field of philology at Wilberforce University.

**Spartacus, a Thracian gladiator, led a revolt of slaves against Roman armies in 73 B.C.

EIGHT

PREPARING FOR YALE
IN IRONWORK

When we reached Talladega after our summer campaign of 1900 I received what was then the greatest surprise of my life, an invitation to speak at the annual meeting of the American Missionary Association to be held in Springfield, Mass., in October. Doctor Beard had read my summer campaign speech, and I was asked to come more than a thousand miles to speak for ten minutes. This invitation gave me my first direct impression of the lofty Christian spirit of the great organization of whose educational work I was a beneficiary. I was a boy of nineteen years, an almost unknown student, and in a position to be commanded. On my way to Springfield I met for the first time Dr. Booker T. Washington, who was likewise invited to speak at the annual meeting. And although the incident has probably never recurred to the mind of that honorable gentleman, I remember that when he learned my mission he shared with me his space in the Pullman car and treated me with such kindly consideration that I was asked by passengers if I was not Mr. Washington's son.

At the Springfield Meeting

The Court Square Theater was packed, and there was an overflow meeting in the church across the street. My speech was lengthened from ten to about twenty minutes at the suggestion of officials who sat upon the platform, the suggestion being made while I spoke. When I crossed the street to speak at the overflow meeting, Doctor Boynton, who presided, said, "If they do this in the green tree, what will they do in the dry?"* The subject of this "green tree" discourse was char-

---

*Luke 23:31.

acteristic of a boy under twenty who had just escaped from the sophomore class, Negro Evolution. But the matter was more practical than
the title. And although I have since enjoyed the enthusiasm of many
occasions where the speaker and his audience become one-hearted and
one-souled, I have never had a more thrilling experience or a more
appreciative audience than the one in the Court Square Theater. Yet
I had heard that Northern audiences were *cold*.

The summer of 1901 gave me an opportunity to learn more of real
Black Belt conditions. I assisted in the summer school work of a Talladega College graduate who founded an institution in a rural community more than ten miles from the nearest railroad station. There
the Negro population greatly preponderates; the Negro owns much of
the land; and next to nothing is done by the authorities of the state
for public instruction. I was impressed by the humanity, the simplicity
and the universal peaceableness of American black folk where they are
left practically to themselves.

I finished at Talladega College in 1902. The old problem of further
education returned. I refused a position in our High School at Little
Rock because I wanted to go to Yale or Harvard. Doctor Andrews, who
seemed to have a perfect confidence in my future, was trying to get
some person of means to assist me at Yale. Dean Henry P. Wright of
Yale, after reading the recommendations of my former teachers, had
written that I could enter the junior class. This great scholar and good
man has been a constant friend since that first acquaintance.

As in former days, I determined to help myself by some decisive
move. Having relatives in Chicago, I thought that I might secure work
in a great city like that; and going thither immediately after my graduation I luckily found an opening in Gates's Ironworks on the north side
of the city among Poles and other foreigners. I was a "helper," supposed
to assist the workmen wherever my services were needed. I was an
apparently unwelcome object to the Poles until they found out that I
could speak German with them. These members of the Catholic faith
were much entertained and amused at my repetitions of German and
mediæval Latin poems to the swinging of my iron sledge. They sought
my company and conversation at noon.

Nine dollars a week for about a dozen weeks will not pay a fellow's
bills at Yale for ten months. But I hoped to save enough to reach New
Haven and support myself for a week or two, at the risk of finding a
chance to earn my board and expenses. Besides, this ironwork gave me
superior physical strength, which is a good part of any preparation for

college. At night I read Carlyle and Emerson, Latin and German, in anticipation of work at Yale. In the middle of the summer I received a word from Doctor Beard of the American Missionary Association in New York, saying, "I am off for Europe, and when I return in the fall I expect to find you at Yale."

The note of that "expectation" sounded like a challenge, and I re-doubled my determination and easily passed by all the huge temptations of a great city. On Sundays I attended Moody's church and the city Young Men's Christian Association. It appeared strange to me that out of 40,000 Negroes I saw no other one at this Young Men's Christian Association during the whole summer.

I became acquainted with Paul Laurence Dunbar, the Negro poet, who was living in Chicago. He cheered me on and wrote encouraging letters until I had finished at Yale. He said that a course at Harvard had always been the unrealized ambition of his life—and how he had earned his breakfasts a few years before by walking seven miles on the hard pavements of Chicago. I was impressed with the possible conse-quences to one who has to battle against the sort of social and economic world that is presented to a black boy in the average Northern city. It might destroy his health and injure his morals. There was pathos in Dunbar's constant praise of the fact that I did not touch any kind of strong drink nor any form of tobacco.

With a faith astonishing to remember I left Chicago in September, settled my preliminary bills at Yale and was enrolled as a junior, with fifteen dollars left in my pocket and the necessity of finding work to earn my board and room. I secured work in the roof garden and res-taurant of the city Young Men's Christian Association, where I could assist the kitchen force in various sorts of work and wash the windows to earn my board. Board is a large and necessary item.

A few days afterwards there came a letter from Mr. D. Stuart Dodge* of New York City saying that he had heard from Doctor Andrews of Talladega College, that I was at Yale, well started, inclosing a check for fifty dollars, and adding that he had one more fifty for my use whenever I should advise him that it was needed. He spoke like a familiar friend, although I had never heard his name before. I put the money in the New Haven Savings Bank and advised the donor, with

---

*David Stuart Dodge (1836–1921), a Yale graduate and former head of the Syrian Protestant College in Beirut.

thanks, that I was earning my board and should certainly not need more money until the beginning of the next term, after Christmas, when tuition bills and new books might bring the need. Something in my letter appealed to the favor of this good man. He sent a second fifty and promised a third fifty upon my request. He read my letter to his aged mother, Mrs. William Dodge, then over ninety years of age, and she insisted that twenty-five dollars additional be sent me on her personal check, with the special direction that it be spent for winter clothes. The thoughtful and sympathetic woman heard that I was from the South. This friend whom I had never seen did even more; he wrote to his cousin, Sec. Anson Phelps Stokes* of Yale University and advised him of my presence among the thousands of that institution. Mr. Stokes pleasantly invited me to command his assistance when I needed it. I could have created the need by stopping the process of earning my board, but I instinctively felt that the work was better.

By their unpatronizing spirit through all of this, these people lifted up and established my respect for mankind. They conferred a blessing upon me as if it were a joy to them, and asked to help me as one might request a favor.

Encouraged and edified by such noble spirits at the start I do not now wonder that I reached upward with body and mind and entered upon two of the most interesting and successful years of all my educational career.

---

*Anson Phelps Stokes (1874–1958), secretary of Yale University and later president of the Phelps-Stokes Fund, a philanthropic organization established in 1911 to aid black education in the U.S. and Africa.

NINE

YALE—THE HENRY JAMES TEN EYCK ORATORICAL CONTEST

My first year at Yale was full of experiences for which former school struggles had in a measure prepared me. After the Christmas examinations, when students are graded for the first term's work, I was classed in Grade A, which according to the policy of the Self-Help Bureau exempted me from payment of tuition, and I stayed in Grade A, never paying another dollar of tuition during my years at Yale. Board I could earn, and other expenses I could manage. A room in White Hall was secured by the kindness of Dean Wright, into whose Latin class I had luckily fallen. After Christmas my Yale studentship was no longer an experiment, and I set out with confidence on the run toward June.

Early in the year there appeared on the bulletin ten subjects for the "Ten Eyck Prize" in oratory. Among them was the simple word, "Hayti." The oration is first written and passed in under an assumed name; there were over three hundred men in my class and about thirty-five passed in papers. Of these the judges chose ten to enter the first speaking contest. At this first speaking five are dropped and five advanced to the final contest. The five who are dropped receive the five third prizes. Of the five who are advanced the successful one will receive the first prize and the four will receive the four second prizes.

I decided to win the first prize. It is a bold thing to acknowledge, but such was my decision. I kept my work at the Young Men's Christian Association until I should see my name among the ten. Once among the ten I felt as sure to win the first prize as I had ever felt that I would master the difficulties of a lesson.

About three weeks before the time for the final contest, which was to take place about the first of April, the "ten" were published and my name appeared with the subject Hayti.

My subsequent plans and decisions seem as audacious to me now as they must to the reader of this narrative. I told my Young Men's Christian Association friends that my name was among the Ten Eyck "ten," and that the first prize would settle my bills for the rest of the year, and that I should win if I gave up extra work and devoted myself to the last three weeks of the contest. "If you do not win," they said, kindly, "you may return." I wrote Doctor Andrews of Talladega College that I was among the ten and that I would be among the "five" at the close of that week. After the preliminary contest I wrote him that I was one of the five and that I would win the first prize two weeks later unless the gods should interfere. I learned later that Doctor Andrews read these missives in public as fast as he received them in the South, and they must have seemed utter audacity to all but him. On April 1 in College Street Hall I was awarded the first prize by the five judges.

My ambition to win was stimulated by a desire to further the acquaintance of other peoples with my race. I had noticed that when I did my classwork among the best, more curiosity was awakened than when a Jew or a Japanese ranked among the best. The surprise with which I was taken struck me as due to a *lack of expectation* in my fellows, and I would succeed in order to cause others to *expect more* of the American Negro.

The Negro students were less than one-half of one per cent. of the three thousand men at Yale. The Negro might not be expected to win often. But judging from the press and personal comment that followed, it would seem that the whole world was a little too much surprised.

But not all that was said and done was prompted by curious surprise rather than positive appreciation. The next morning I found in the Yale post office a check for fifty dollars with appreciation from the Yale Glee, Banjo and Mandolin Clubs Association. For weeks there came daily twenty-five or more appreciative letters. Mrs. Corinne Roosevelt Robinson, sister of the President, had never quite forgotten me since my little summer campaign speech in 1900, and she sent Godspeed and a personal check. One of the most highly appreciated letters came from ex-Pres. Grover Cleveland. A good lady of Newport gave me my first and only diamond pin. There came through the mails from New York City three fifty-dollar gold certificates in an anonymous letter signed by "An Unknown Well-wisher." It contained half a dozen words, the briefest and the fullest missive ever sent me. I remembered the text that begins "Unto him that hath."*

---

*See Luke 8:18.

So many good and sensible letters were bound to be offset by some others of more or less eccentric ideas and suggestions. Some organization in Kentucky, which seemed from their literature to have had some designs on Hayti for some time, wrote me a proposal that they would seize the island by some sort of filibustering expedition from the United States if I would accept the presidency. Shades of Dessalines and Toussaint L'Ouverture!* I had no desire to add to the volcanic little government's already too numerous chief executives.

The appreciation of my classmates was generous. When my name was seen among the ten, there was a mixture of amused and sympathetic interest. The proportion of amusement was overdone only by one Jew who was an unsuccessful aspirant for the honor and who referred to me among the boys as "the black Demosthenes."** I told him it would have been more Jewlike for him to say black David, or black Jacob. When I entered the five, I was taken more seriously. And when I won the final contest there was a burst of generous and manly enthusiasm.

I never like to describe human ugliness for its own sake, but there was one fellow who is worth describing because he is such a good illustration of a type—not a Yale type, but a type of man. Among the best and seemingly sincerest of my Yale friends were some boys from the South, especially from the freedom-loving hills of the border states. But there was one fellow from the state school of my own state. We entered Yale together and he, knowing me to be a Southern Negro fighting for my very existence, was at first very, very patronizing. He would "hello" me a block away, inquire with a half amused, half good-natured smile "how I was making it?" and make every effort of bland superiority. I uniformly and politely accepted all his good advances, never seeking them. Soon my classmates began to talk on the campus about my work. He became less friendly—I had to be nearer to him than the distance of a block to get a "hello." After the Christmas "exams" the boys had tales to tell; how I walked out from nearly every

---

*François Dominique Toussaint L'Ouverture (c. 1744–1803) led a successful slave revolt in Haiti and after conquering Santo Domingo in 1801 became ruler of the entire island. After Toussaint was treacherously deposed by a French expedition in 1802, one of his generals, Jean-Jacques Dessalines (c. 1758–1806), led a campaign that threw out the French invaders. On January 1, 1804, Dessalines proclaimed Haitian independence and was chosen governor for life.
**Demosthenes (383–322 B.C.) was an Athenian statesman generally regarded as the greatest of the ancient Greek orators.

examination when most of them were not half through. Then he hardly spoke when he met me face to face; I tried hard to be uniform and unconscious of change. Next day after the oratorical contest I met him squarely on the street, and as I was about to give the friendly greeting he pulled down his hat over his eyes and passed as one passes a lamp-post.

People naturally ask how I fared during my next year, my senior year, at Yale. A month before my graduation I was invited to address the State Congregational Association of Illinois, and when a minister of that body asked me that question I told the story of a Negro woman in the South who believed in "voodooism." Her husband was fussy and disagreeable, so she went to the "conjure doctor" to get a remedy for the old man's distemper. The conjurer gave her a bottle of clear liquid, and directed that when the "fuss" started in the house she must take a mouthful of it herself, and added his particular direction that it must not be swallowed under a quarter of an hour after being taken into the mouth. She followed directions and the vicarious treatment completely cured the old man. Returning to the doctor in astonishment she asked what the remedy could be, and he replied: "Cold water—but it kept *your* tongue still!"

But there is nothing more generous and noble than the heart of a boy, and young men are but "boys grown tall." During my senior year they acknowledged my right to a part of their world. They never quite got away from the surprise that "you do your lessons as well as anybody!" While crossing the campus at examination times I was often stopped by a crowd of fellows who had just finished some examination. They would hand me the list of questions, and as I answered them they would say, "I made it," or "I failed," according as their answers had agreed or disagreed with mine. "Pickens, you ought to be a lawyer!" shouted one fellow after I had gone through such a list of questions from our five-hour law course. I could hardly have registered to vote in that fellow's state.

At graduation time I was ranked in the "Philosophical Oration" group of the class who are credited with "honors in all studies." I had been with the class two years, just the time required to merit a Phi Beta Kappa Key if one's scholarship warrants it. So much was printed and said about my admission to this society that a clear statement might correct some error. It was said that my admission was opposed. Well, a great university is much like the outside world; it holds many different spirits. No one should be surprised at differences of opinion in a *university*. In our senior year a resolution was introduced in the Phi Beta Kappa Society that no one be admitted to membership that year except such as began as Freshmen. I entered Yale as a Junior; but there is no way of determining that this was a "grandfather clause"* inspired by my presence. A few fellows tried mischievously to impress me that the legislation was in my honor, but I consistently and persistently refused to acknowledge it—and somehow the resolution proved ineffective and I was awarded a key. The Phi Beta Kappa Society is based on scholarship, and Yale is a very democratic community.

After-word

After Yale, what? A famous lecture bureau of New York City laid before me a tempting contract to be carted around over Europe and America for three years as a sort of lecture-curiosity. I had been invited to speak before various dignified gatherings, at Newport, Hartford and at the annual banquet of the Citizens' Trades Association of Cambridge, Mass. But after seeking and finding good advice in the secretary of Yale University, the secretary of the American Missionary Association and Paul Laurence Dunbar who had tried the curiosity-show business, I decided that show-lecturing would be of doubtful influence on my future—although it would have given me an opportunity to accomplish one of the desires of every college man, a visit to the Old World.

The work of education seemed to offer a greater field of usefulness to a Negro than any other profession. My own school struggles emphasized this thought. Back to the South was my inclination. That section is big with the destiny of the American Negro, and therefore with the future of the Negro race in the whole world. After considering the timely offers of various educational authorities, including those of Tuskegee and the American Missionary Association, I decided to begin work in the American Missionary Association College at Talladega, Ala., where I have been teacher of languages since leaving Yale in

---

*An ironic reference to laws enacted between 1895 and 1910 in a number of southern states restricting the right to vote to those descended from persons who had the right to vote as of January 1, 1867. The so-called grandfather clause was declared unconstitutional by the U.S. Supreme Court in 1915.

1904. My experience of the usefulness of this institution, as well as gratitude for the greatest of benefits, made this decision logical and good.

On my way from New England to Talladega a visit to the World's Exposition in St. Louis brought me by Little Rock, Ark., and the scenes and memories of public-school days, the "skiff-ferry" and the "stave factory"—and the colored citizens and a few white friends gave me the biggest and most pleasant reception of all my life.

In the last six years it has been impossible for me to supply all the demands upon my energies as a lecturer or speaker at institutions and gatherings. I have visited nearly all of the important Negro schools of the South, and it has given me a good look into the condition and needs of my people. In 1906 I took up Esperanto, and after a correspondence with Esperantists all over the world, I was awarded a diploma by the British Esperanto Association. In 1908 Fisk University honored me with the degree of Master of Arts.

In 1905 I met the most helpful and the most enduring good fortune of all my life, the traditional and the real "best woman in the world." Miss Minnie Cooper McAlpine, who like myself was a product of the American Missionary Association work, had graduated at Tougaloo University in Mississippi and taught for three years in the American Missionary Association school at Meridian. Since this meeting there have come in succession three of the brightest and best joys that high heaven lends to earth, William, Jr., Hattie Ida and Ruby Annie.

These latter years have a history of their own—which can be better written, perhaps, when they are seen through a perspective of years. Had I written of my boyhood experiences right on the heels of their passage, I could not have presented them in their truer light and proportion. The distance of years lends not merely enchantment but sobriety to the view.

To advance your life is but to push forward the front of your battle to find the same inspiriting struggle still. Oh, the blessing of a boyhood that trains to endurance and struggle! To do the best one can, wherever placed, is a summary of all the rules of success. When I was in the public school of Argenta, Ark., I one day missed a word in the spelling class, the only word I missed during the five years, and a word that I could easily have spelled. The teacher took quick advantage of the careless trick of my brain and passed the word on to my neighbor without giving me the usual second trial, saying as he did so that a boy who had never missed a word had no right ever to miss a word. He wished, no doubt, to punish carelessness. That one missed word was more talked of among my fellows than all the hundreds of words I had spelled, and I was taught the lesson that the man who succeeds is never conceded the right to fail.

I have learned that righteousness and popularity are not always yoke-fellows, and sometimes run a contrary course. From early boyhood I was laughed at among my fellows for the contemptible weakness of totally abstaining from strong drink and tobacco, while in my manhood the best of my fellows commend the abstention as a virtue. I have learned the uplifting lesson that the real heart of humanity appreciates manhood above things; as a copperless struggler I was often accorded a place above the possessor of gold. I have been impressed, not that every single thought and deed in the world is good, but that the resultant line of humanity's movement is in the direction of righteousness, and that human life and the world are on the whole good things.

BURSTING BONDS

TEN

COLLEGE TEACHER

When the preceding chapters of this story were written, I was busy with my first job after graduating from Yale. As a teacher in Talladega College I had had just seven years in the battle of real life. Real living is the great educator. When the student views life through the curricula of his school, it has a rather ideal appearance. Viewed from the pinnacle of some great university, life is like the world seen from an airplane: all the structures and highways, plots and plottings of man, seen from the air, have an artistic and picturesque appearance,—even the very crookednesses are toned into charming lines. When a fellow's plane is sailing over some great city, for example, he may see only its distant sky-line, the beauty of its surrounding landscapes and the magnificence of its more prominent structures. He will not hear the shrieks of its murders; he will not see the gauntness of its hunger; he will not smell the reeking of its sewers. As the panorama passes beneath him, he can have no suggestion of a child being trampled, a maiden seduced, a man butchered, or a bank robbed. He senses the charm of the topography and the wonder of the works of organized human society.

For ten years I toiled at Talladega College. I learned much. It was the period of that institution's most rapid development. Mrs. Pickens, who had brought along into life one of the voices of the angels, sang in its choirs and choruses, and lullabied her three babies at home. She was a volunteer worker, without pay. I was paid the usual Southern-Negro-missionary-college-teacher's salary. Most of the teachers were white. In the ten years we saw a great procession of these teachers come and go,—some came to teach the Negro, but a few came principally to spend the winter in a warmer climate. Most of them were faithful to their tasks. Some of them were at best a hindrance to the advancement of the Negro race. Among the great teachers were George W. Andrews, who presided over the institution for eight years, as successor to its first president, Henry S. DeForest; William E. Hutchison, who

was dean of the college during my student days; Edwin C. Silsby, secretary and treasurer, who spent thirty-five or forty years in the most
devoted service man ever rendered to man; Esther A. Barnes, teacher
of literature and history, who would have graced a similar chair in any
New England college; and Annetta C. Bruce, who lived and died for
the girlhood of a race not her own.

One of the greatest drawbacks to these missionary enterprises is the
absentee control, and the consequent necessity for dealing with the
whole situation through one man, sometimes, by accident, a very little
man. The controlling boards of these institutions consisted chiefly of
New Yorkers and New Englanders, who had no intimate acquaintance
either with the schools or with the life of the pupils who attended them.
At Yale it is different: the corporation are Yale graduates, and the
faculty are Yale scholars, or scholars from Harvard or some other school
comparable with Yale. But the trustees of the missionary colleges know
only *about* them, and it is one of the handicaps of such absentee authority that it must get its information and its slant on the situation
from some man whom it has on the job. This man is usually, but not
always, the president of the school. When he is a white man, he is
almost sure to choose in his turn some Negro of a usable type, through
whom the white man will make all of his mental contacts and formulate
most of his opinions concerning the whole Negro race. Among the
personnel of such a drama a large role will be played by individual
whim, petty jealousy, envy and other human weaknesses.

An arrangement wherein a narrow and small-minded man is put in
a position of authority over larger-spirited and broader-minded men, is
one of the most annoying things in this world—*for the little man in
charge.* The bigger men can stand to be under him much better than
he can stand to be over them. Another trouble-breeding element in
such a situation is the law of American white people, a law unwritten
but seldom disobeyed by them, that wherever white people and colored
people work together in such enterprises, even in those that are pro-
fessedly for the special benefit of the Negro race, the whites must occupy
the highest places, regardless of other qualifications. For instance, if a
young white man comes into such a work and shows extraordinary
ambition and capacity for attainment, he creates a problem, but the
problem can be solved in the normal way, by promoting him; but a
young colored man of like qualities, in that he cannot be promoted,
creates an unsolvable problem. The result is the strange contradiction

of a man *too well fitted to suit.* So that in America we can have the phenomenon of a Negro paid to act, but too active to please; hired to do, but who *does too much.* This is not fiction. I have heard the anomalous complaint made against a young Negro teacher that he was "too popular" with the student body, and that his influence and popularity among the colored population in general and among the unsophisticated white patrons of the institution had become an embarrassment to the president. The only solution of such a difficulty in America is either to turn the whole institution over to Negro workers, thereby making promotion normal among them, or—to move the individual Negro.

When I left Yale and went to Talladega College as a teacher, some of the pupils in my classes were older than I, many of them having been my fellow-students before I went to Yale. But I will never have any dearer memory than that of the respect, the devotion and the love of these students. For those reasons, doubtless, I got more hours of work out of them than most of the other teachers could get. I was not known as a "soft" teacher: until this day I hear many amusing reminiscences among Talladega graduates, of my awful driving energies, of my uncompromising, and perhaps unreasonable, insistence upon minute punctuality by the face of the clock, and my Mede-and-Persian laws about minimum period of study for each subject. I was even accused (by some of the other teachers) of being too hard on the students, while the students confided in me with a wholeheartedness which must have been a puzzlement to other members of the faculty. My only explanation for this is, that the students believed that, right or wrong in fact, I was sincere in purpose; and so, whatever they disagreed with in my driving harshness, they condoned and excused as a mistaken notion of mine in the pursuit of their best good. A conviction of sincerity transforms the quality of an act. Before either of us realized it, therefore, the student had formed a regular habit of confiding in me both his individual and his group difficulties, and of seeking my advice in every kind of situation.

This was not because I was black. There were other colored teachers in whom the students had no confidence whatever. Of all people on earth students are the quickest to observe any kow-towing and truckling on the part of a teacher to the "powers that be."

The truth ought to be told bravely, if anything is told. Because of the peculiar genius which has been developed in the white-and-black relationship in America, even the good, conscientious, missionary white people are likely to find a really straight-out, straight-up, manly and self-respecting Negro coworker *inconvenient* at times, to say the least. All the greater credit to the few white Americans who in all circumstances manage to live up to their democratic and Christian professions. Life forced upon me, or developed within me, the habit of thinking for myself, so that I have never been afraid to stand alone,— too little afraid perhaps. I have never had a disposition to imitate any authority, either in writing an essay, making a speech, getting a lesson into a pupil,—or sketching an autobiography. It is possible for such a black man to be sometimes something of a trial to a white man reared in the United States.—In this connection it ought to be recorded that in the communities where I have lived the better classes of the white people professed a respect and a degree of liking for me. As is characteristic of southern white people, they showed this indirectly by their attitude toward me in their shops and on the streets, and by remarks casually dropped in the presence of their colored maids and house-boys: "We like him because he does not try to fool us about his way of thinking. He does not pretend to agree with us,—but he minds his own business." By the same indirect methods they would say (to their colored people) that they resented the fact that some of the northern white teachers tried to impress the southern white by pretending to see things from the southern point of view. Southerners are suspicious of a northerner who pretends, in conversation with them on the streets and in the stores, to adopt the southern viewpoint, while the northerner continues to teach Negroes in a Negro college. And there is reason in such suspicion.

Meanwhile I was still in great demand as a speaker before all sorts of groups, white and colored, who were interested in the "Negro problem," but especially before church and religious organizations of the North and East, which were interested in Negro education.

Early in the century William Edward Burghardt Du Bois, of Atlanta University, had formed the "Niagara Movement,"* by getting together the few liberal-minded Negro men who in that perilous time dared to have thoughts of their own about their own, and who were foolhardy

----

*William Edward Burghardt Du Bois (1868–1963), the most influential African American thinker and writer of the twentieth century, launched the Niagara Movement in 1905. A national civil rights organization of approximately 400 members, the Niagara Movement anticipated the National Association for the Advancement of Colored People.

enough to run the risk of the great crime of being called "radicals." I had become a member of this organization, which was the first national movement of colored people with a primary regard for their equal citizenship. The immediate heir and successor of that organization is the one now known as the National Association for the Advancement of Colored People.

It was therefore natural that a desire should arise among those who controlled Talladega College to "promote" me suddenly, by taking me out of my professorship there and sending me to the "headmastership" of a minor school in another State, with an advance in pay. Only I preferred not to be so promoted, and taking a choice of my own I began in another college at a lower salary than what I had received when I started teaching ten years previously.—Before coming to that, however, I will recall in the next chapter an experience which I had long looked forward to, and which I had before leaving Talladega.

ELEVEN

TOUR OF EUROPE

In the summer of 1913, one year before the outbreak of the World War, Mrs. Pickens and I, accompanied by our friend, Mrs. Flora E. Avery, of Galesburg, Illinois, had a wonderful tour of Europe, when the pre-war civilization of Britain and the Continent was at its pinnacle. We made a tour of England, Wales and Scotland, and of most of the states of the Continent. It is the duty of every human to see as much of the rest of the world as possible. And readers of human history have an inner urge toward the older places of mankind.

I was about to go alone and had applied for ship passage; for Mrs. Pickens, like most good women, had thought that it would "cost too much" for her to go, and that it was "more important" that I should go while she stayed to look after the babies and the home. Good fortune, however, brought me early in the year to see my friend, the Reverend Dr. George Whitfield Andrews, at his place of retirement in Oberlin. This was the same man who had written me fourteen years before that I could "have hope," and who had graciously accepted three little ten dollar bills as collateral for my whole college education. When I now told him of my plans to see the best of Europe, his first question was: "Will your wife go?" And when I explained her attitude in the matter, he advised: "Take your wife. She perhaps thinks you cannot afford to take her, but you can less afford not to take her. The trip will mean a thousand times more: for not only in Europe but in later years you can live the trip over and over again if your wife shares in it. The *only* thing to do, is to take her."—I took his advice, and I want to pass it on to all other men. Mrs. Pickens proved to be selective genius of the whole trip. Certainly I saw a hundredfold more of the "old masters" of art and beauty and architecture, than my own uncomplemented tastes would ever have led me to see. We had a complete set of Baedeker *

---

* Baedeker's guide and travel books to Europe were widely used by American tourists.

and would acquaint ourselves beforehand with every by-path which we were about to take, through the Trossachs in Scotland or down the Tell Lakes in Switzerland. In addition to this, Mrs. Pickens would read some good novel concerning that particular castle or palace or region.

Mrs. Flora E. Avery, our friend of Galesburg, Illinois, and an unapologetic friend of Negro education and advancement, accompanied us. The three made an ideal tourist party: we could always see whatever we wanted to see and stay as long as we pleased. If we hired a guide, he served our wishes. We were not hurried along and pulled away, as members of large tourist parties are. In America we bought only our passage from Montreal to Liverpool, and our return accommodations from Naples to Boston. We could therefore take our own time at Niagara, through the Thousand Islands and down the St. Lawrence River. After sightseeing in Liverpool and its neighborhood and in Wales, we journeyed on through the region of the English Lakes and through Scotland, and down from Edinburgh through the great manufacturing cities to London. We tarried in London, taking side trips to the historic places thereabout: the palaces of the kings and nobles and the seats of fame. Everywhere we visited the grand operas, the theatres, the art galleries, the museums, the gardens and parks, the beautiful lakes and the great mountains. Having the company of Mrs. Pickens and Mrs. Avery made me always take the better accommodations, and so I got more out of it. And I have never spent money more profitably.

Leaving England we took the nauseating Channel passage to France, via Dover and Calais. We tarried as long as possible in Paris, enjoying the beauty and art of its Louvre, the wonders of its towers and gardens and boulevards, and the extravagance of Versailles, where Louis XIV bankrupted a nation. Then on we journeyed through the Netherlands, battled again at Napoleon's Waterloo, saw the beautiful laces being made by underpaid girls in Brussels, and the ivory extorted from maimed black people in the Congo, much of this ivory being carved into little crucified "Christs" for the adoration of the pious. We experienced the quaintness and the cleanness of Holland and the awful smell of its canals, saw the queer islanders who dress in the styles of generations ago, the "Peace Palace" and the Dutch Masters of painting.

It was summer. The kings were away on their vacations. So everywhere we strode through the kings' palaces, tipping the caretakers, and we stretched on the lounges and sat in the seats of royalty for the fun of it,—seats often much less comfortable than the seats at home.

We traversed the beautiful Rhine, with its numberless castles and castle ruins of the days of the robber knights and barons, when each robber evidently tried to build his own house so high on the mountain and so thick of wall that the others could not rob him back. Then we traversed the country of Luther and the great cities of Germany, tarrying longest in Berlin. This proved to be the best ordered city we saw, and it is fair to record that in 1913 there was more evidence of virility in Germany than in any other nation we visited, even England. And it was plain that war was inevitable between France and Germany. They were both "toting guns" for each other, Germany having the better gun and the more practiced skill. From Berlin we visited Potsdam and Sans Souci, the seat of Frederick the Great, and Charlottenburg, and as Wilhelm II was out of town, we examined his palace.

We traveled on through the centers of art and government in Saxony and Bavaria, looking the Sistine Madonna in the face at Dresden, touching Austria at Innsbruck, and entering Switzerland,—Switzerland which must always be in the singular number,—passing through the country of Wilhelm Tell and climbing the heaven-buttressing Alps right on up to the pinnacle of the sky on the glaciers and snows of the Jungfrau. Down to Lake Geneva and through the Simplon Tunnel,— for *through* the Alps lies Italy, as Hannibal would now find. In a few minutes a train rolls under the Alps where formerly it took dangerous days to cross.

In Italy were Milan and Venice and Florence and Rome, the Eternal, and Naples and its Bay indescribable. When I visited some of these places for the first time, I seemed to have a vague recollection that I had visited them before: localities in England, the "Tell Lakes" in Switzerland, the Forum at Rome and Mount Vesuvius. When in school, I often came to a new proposition or theorem in science or mathematics with a more or less distinct feeling that I had learned it before, some-time, somewhere. There is certainly a "transmigration of the soul" through literature and art. As we sailed through the Four Forest Canton Lakes, I could point out to myself the places of Tell's exploits. And the only thing wanting in the Forum at Rome was for Caesar or Cicero to pass by, for Antonius or Catilina to stroll past with his retainers or loiter along with his gangsters, or a victorious legion to rush in from Gaul or Africa.—The Amalfi Drive, the Island of Capri, and Pompeii, the exhumed "city of the dead," are scenes unforgettable.

From Naples we sailed back over the blue Mediterranean, and out through the gates of Hercules, stopping ashore at the Azores Islands and reaching Boston after a fourteen-days' trip.

Not all American white people are alike, but it is noteworthy that on all this journey during all these months the only snobs we met, were some of our fellow-Americans. Mrs. Avery is white and Mrs. Pickens light of skin, so that my face served as the only cue to these snobs. Being far from Mississippi and Texas, they could not work their will, but they often showed their manners anyhow, just from sheer force of habit. Strange truth it is, that whenever any person tried to insult us, we knew at once that he or she was not one of our potential "enemies" but one of our fellow-patriots. Often we would never have been able to discover his identity and our relation to him, if only he had been able to control his feelings. Whenever any one glared as we entered a dining-room, or tried to spread himself out over three or four seats when we entered a vehicle, we knew where he was from. And those who made the biggest scenes, proved, on investigation, to be from the section of the United States where they are *most used to colored folk*, where from infancy they sit in the laps and eat out of the hands of black people. If a fellow was from Mississippi, where he had slept in the bed and suckled at the breast of a black nurse, he made the biggest fuss of anybody. Some of it was ludicrous. We had great fun. In that summer Jack Johnson was just running away from the American police,* so in Belgium and Naples they took me for him.—A black person, a white-colored person, and a white person together make a combination fit for any experience.

When we have just learned how to begin to live, we die. One year after my return from Europe I had completed just ten years as a teacher in Talladega College, and was certainly ten times better prepared for that position than when I was first elected to it,—and I found myself leaving it. In my last two years in Alabama I was president of the Alabama State Teachers' Association, of colored educators, and had many a cordial day with Booker T. Washington. Since I was nineteen years old, we had repeatedly found ourselves together as speakers on many large occasions, North and South. I introduced him in his last important address in Birmingham and Montgomery, Alabama, and pre-

---

*Jack Johnson (1878–1946), heavyweight champion of the world from 1908 to 1915, fled to Europe in 1913 to avoid serving a penitentiary sentence for violating the Mann Act.

sided at the banquet closing the last of his "state tours" in Shreveport, Louisiana.

From Talladega College I went as head of the department of Greek and sociology, to Wiley University, at Marshall, Texas,—to Texas! In the next chapter I shall record some of the experience of my one eventful year there. During the year I was elected to the deanship of another college.—My acquaintanceship and contact with the general public had been increasing steadily since I was a boy.

TWELVE

WILEY UNIVERSITY
AND TEXAS

As Talladega College, in Alabama, is an enterprise of the Congregational Church for the education of the Negro, so Wiley University, at Marshall, Texas, is an enterprise of the Northern Methodist Episcopal Church.* The town of Marshall is not far from the southern border of Arkansas and only forty miles from Shreveport, Louisiana,—one of the worst sections in all this round world, certainly for any Negro to live in. A complete statement of the unhappy situation and savage treatment of colored people in this section of the civilized world would not be believed by any one who has not had personal experience with it. I shall, therefore, not strain credulity too far by endeavoring to tell the whole truth, but will relate only some of the believable things.

Wiley University had the reputation of being the largest and most advanced Negro college west of the Mississippi River, and it was living up well to its reputation. Looking across a valley from the campus of Wiley University, one can see the plant of another well reputed Negro institution, Bishop College, maintained by Northern Baptists. The president of Bishop and a part of its teaching force were white people. The president of Wiley and all of his teachers were colored, with the exception of several lady teachers in the girls' industrial home, which while co-operating with Wiley was really under the separate control of the women's missionary organizations of the Methodist Episcopal Church North.

In spite of the convincing testimony of these two important Negro institutions of learning and their long and honorable history, the white population of the town and county had not yet conceded a human

---

*Wiley University was founded in 1873 and chartered in 1882 by the Freedmen's Aid Society, which later became the Board of Education of the United Methodist Church.

status to the colored people, who greatly outnumbered the white. In addition to the usual oppression of Jim Crowism, disfranchisement, segregation and the denial of public accommodation and privilege, colored individuals were visited with occasional beating and bullying in the highways and the awful terror of lynching. We hate to record any of it here in this little history which is delightful to us in its many vicissitudes which, though bitter in the passage, are pleasant in the memory.

The colored president of Wiley University was (and, as we write, still is) Matthew W. Dogan, who at that time had already spent a score of years in the position. The general public will never be able to appreciate the self-sacrifice and self-control necessary in such a situation. To be the executive of a school grudgingly supported by a distant missionary sentiment, is one thing. But it is quite another thing to bring up one's children to a fair degree of education and culture in the face of a terror which unceasingly denies them the primary recognition and the elemental expression of self-respect. The most prominent colored woman of the place was denied the right to answer a call over the long-distance telephone from her husband, because when she answered the operator's query, she replied, naturally and without premeditation: "Yes, this is Mrs.————." And because she called herself "Mrs.," she was not allowed to talk over that phone.

Wiley and Bishop have much athletic rivalry. When the Wiley girls and their chaperons and other teachers, on their way to Bishop, were passing through the street by the white high school, some of the white pupils came out and threw stones at the passers-by, while the high school teachers stood in the background, indifferently looking on. A colored professor of one of the colleges, who is well known and respected among his people in the State, was without provocation beaten into unconsciousness by two whites, and all that "the good white people" of the town did about it, was to visit the bedside of the victim (a very exceptional attention, of course), where he was laid up for weeks, and advise him that it was "best not to try to do anything about it," as that would make more trouble, and to assure him that the sympathies of "the good white people" (including the bankers and merchants with whom he did business) were with him and not with the scoundrels who had beaten him up. Meanwhile the scoundrels were not in the least annoyed or inconvenienced.

In the January of my year at Wiley University one of the college boys, a fine and trustworthy fellow, who drove the president's carriage and did chores for the president in the town, selected for that position because he was polite, tactful, level-headed, and would know how to get along through the streets of this dangerous community, was shot up by the "pound officer," who emptied his six-shooter at the boy, wounding him in the legs. This is why: while the boy was driving the president's carriage, a vehicle well known to all the whites of the town, keeping close to the right-hand curb, the pound officer came from the opposite direction in his buggy, staying right in the middle of the street, so that his buggy just barely touched the vehicle driven by the boy. Neither vehicle was injured in the slightest, and so light was the touch that the boy barely perceived it, as he drove along laughing and talking to another boy on the seat beside him. The officer simply stepped out of his buggy and emptied his gun at the back of the body of this boy. "Damn nigger! trying to run over me."—"If a damn nigger tried to run over me, I'd shoot him, too!" was what the officer of the law said, when he came out to the college to see about it,—really to see what anybody at the college proposed to try to do about it.—This was so horrible that the good white people actually succeeded in getting the criminal indicted, tried and lightly fined,—but he took an "appeal," and that was the last we heard of it.

Even the sordid motives of greed and gain found it hard to survive race prejudice in Marshall. The colored people of "New Town," a segregated section on the other side of the university from the main town, found it at first impossible and always difficult to get telephones and electric lights installed in their homes. Such conveniences were too good for colored folk. Only after a long time and very grudgingly were these luxuries allowed to penetrate this pale. And as for pavements, street lights, sewers and sanitary improvements, these they simply could not get, for greed and gain did not fight on the side of the Negro, but rather against him, in these tax-paid services.

I could easily understand the reasonableness and timeliness of the program of a new organization that had been started in New York in 1909 with the avowed aim of bettering the condition of the American Negro. It takes experience to make one understand clearly. I had become a member of this organization when it opened its membership books, and many times from Alabama or Texas I traveled thousands of miles, in painful "Jim Crow" for most of the distance, answering a call to address some great meeting which this new force, known as the

National Association for the Advancement of Colored People, was staging in the North or East. This I regarded as entirely consistent with the large service which I was privileged to render for the educational interests in which I was employed. This was not always the viewpoint of my employers. They never risked, however, such precarious methods as argument or reason, but always some indirect pressure. They could not say that fighting lynching was inconsistent with fighting ignorance, or that the N.A.A.C.P. was too radical an ally for so conservative a thing as philanthropy-supported religious education, but they tried to "show" me by hampering rules, various inconveniences and disfavors. I must confess: that I always understood them thoroughly,—and that I always refused to understand any of these substitutes for reason. Matthew W. Dogan, the only Negro president with whom I have worked, was the only school head who seemed to understand and to endorse my larger relations to the affairs of colored people, and not to fear the public's interest in me. "The more you can do," said he, "the better."— It takes a man who lives the life, to understand.

The northeastern part of Texas, at least, is still, for the Negro race, all that "Bill" Sherman's metaphor made it out to be.* And before I leave this twelvemonth tussle with Texas, I wish to tell, as modestly as the truth about them can be told, of two incidents, one as the conclusion of this chapter and the other as the next chapter,—incidents illustrative of the peril of a colored man in such a civilization, if he be inconvenienced by self-respect.

In the town of Marshall a white man owed me six dollars and a few cents, in an insurance transaction. It was six months or more before he paid me, and this is what happened in the meanwhile. First, he promised to send the amount as soon as he could hear from the head office. I made a note on my calendar about six weeks ahead. When that leaf of the calendar turned up, having not heard from him, I sent a simple card of inquiry and received a reply that the head office had not yet been heard from. I marked the memorandum six weeks further ahead. And so on for several months. Then he changed his method a bit: he no longer wrote anything but would send the colored boy, about thirteen years old, a servant, with the message: "Mr. A———tol' me

---

*Perhaps a reference to Gen. William Tecumseh Sherman's remark that "war is hell" or General Philip Sheridan's observation that if he owned hell and Texas, he'd rent out Texas and go live in hell.

to tell yer that he'll sen' yer the money next month." And so on for a while.

Finally one morning as I ate my breakfast, the colored lad turned up in my front door with the announcement: "P'fesser Pickens, Mr. A———sez he will sen' yer the money Sat'day." It was then Monday, and as I had sent no recent reminder, I regarded this unsolicited announcement as very auspicious. Truth is, hope of collection had been so often deferred that it had disappeared.

But immediately I found myself face to face with the most vicious, cowardly and dangerous element in the whole southern situation. For in all this transaction I had had nothing whatever to do with any woman, had not seen any woman. I had dealt with a middle-aged white man, and with no other person, man or woman. But next day after the colored boy came to my door with the announcement, I was called over the phone and when I answered, a woman's voice was at the other end:

"Is that Pickens?"

"This is he."

"Well, this is Mrs. A———. We sent you that money two or three months ago by 'General'," their nickname for the colored lad, "an' he's been working for us a long time an' he's honest an' he always does just what we tell him an' we trust him an' he says he gave you the money"———.

At this lull in her speech I replied: "There may be some mistake. The boy was at our house yesterday to say that Mr. A———would pay the money Saturday."

"I don't see how he could do that, he was here 'til time for school,— an' besides, the money had already been sent to you long ago."

"That's strange. I did not get the money. And he came to the door as we ate breakfast yesterday morning and said that the money would be sent Saturday."

"Didn't you get that money?"

"I did not get the money." ("No" or "Yes" would have been too abrupt.)

"Well, he said you were away with the college baseball team and he gave the money to your wife."

"I never go away with the baseball teams."—And I began to think of the wolf and the lamb who were drinking out of the same stream: the lamb was attacked and eaten for "muddying the water" for the wolf, although the wolf was *upstream* from the lamb.—"O, did you send a check?"

"No. We sent the money,—we always send money by 'General,'—an' he's honest,—we've always trusted him," etc.

"Well, I will go and ask Mrs. Pickens. But I am sure she did not get it, for she heard the boy say yesterday morning that it would be sent Saturday."

I spoke to Mrs. Pickens. She had not only heard the boy's message the day before, but had heard him many times before announcing future dates when Mr. A——would close the transaction. So, to be rid of the matter, I simply returned to the telephone and announced that Mrs. Pickens had not received the money.—It should be noticed that I showed no feeling in the matter whatever, and made no insistence or suggestion that the money should ever be paid. I thought I was through with it.

"Well, when you are down town to-morrow, you come in here and see us about it.—If 'General' spent that money we'll take it out of his wages Saturday.—Maybe he gave it to some other woman that looks like your wife.—You stop in here to-morrow."

"You might ask the boy about it and settle it up with him. All we know is we never got the money."—I never intended to "stop in," and I had better sense than to say I never intended to do so. I had never seen that woman. I meant never to see her.

It should be noticed that I did not fall into any little trap. I did not "sass" this white woman. I did not even say "no" or "yes" to her, and yet I did not say "No, Ma'am" or "Yes, Ma'am." I did not notice her implications that I was trying to be paid twice, and I did not call her a liar, even indirectly. I made no implications. I did not say or show: that I had had no dealing with her, that I had never seen her, that it was none of her business, and that Mr. A——should speak to me about the matter. No, I did not "insult a white woman," as I might have been expected to do.

Several days passed. I forgot the matter, as I never expected the money after that. When hope is lost, interest is lost. But as we played in a tennis tournament on the campus, I was informed by some of the students that an auto had stopped in front of my house and that some one evidently wanted to see me. Going toward the machine and observing a white man and a white woman, I greeted them politely. I had never seen either of them before and could not connect them with any affairs of mine. Hanging up behind on the roadster was a colored boy, whom I had not observed yet. So I waited for a moment with some curiosity to learn their business. The man said nothing. The woman spoke.

"I am Mrs. A———, an' this is my son, a lawyer, an' we have come to see about that money we sent you."

I was on my guard.—"Well———." Still looking, I said only that one word, but with an inflection which meant: I am ready and willing to have a settlement.

Then in a more aggressive and less friendly tone she continued: "We've brought 'General' here, an' he says he paid that money."

I looked at the boy: "Why this is the boy who came the other day and said that Mr. A———had instructed him to say that he would send the money Saturday."

Then for the first time the young white man spoke up: "Come 'round here, 'General'."—The boy came drooping around, looking down, as if unable to face anybody. The lawyer proceeded to ask the 'General' some direct questions, which sounded like a rehearsal:

"Did you come up here Monday?"

"Naw-Sir."

"Did you say the money would be sent Saturday?"

"Naw-Sir."

"Did you give 'em that money?"

"Yaas-Sir."

My first reaction was that the boy had stolen and was trying thus to cover the theft. I said to the child: "Son, I wouldn't lie and soil my soul even it I lost my job."

Then the real purpose and temper of this little mission showed itself. The white man snarled: "Don't you try to bully him! That money was given to you an' we are not going to have any big talk!"

To this I replied hotly, of course: "Wait a minute! Which of us is trying the 'bullying'? Who owes the money? To whom is the money due? Where is the evidence of its payment? Have I bothered you for it? Have I come to see you about it, or have you come to see me? I thought you came to *find out*. We have not got the money. The boy is lying."

Then a ludicrous thing happened, which almost made me laugh out, in spite of the situation. The white man leaned over toward me and said under his breath, with a threatening gleam in his eye: "Well, don't you talk so loud!" Why did he say that? Because by that time all the colored people around had come as near as they dared—to listen. And a Texas white man, of all disgraces, was most ashamed for colored people, whom he had bullied often before, to hear some new-comer Negro talking back to him defiantly.

I understood his predicament but did not act upon the hint. And in an effort to "save his face" he did a desperate thing, which usually works in Texas: he threatened me with bodily harm on the spot: "I am going to get out o' this car and smash your face!" He made a quick stage movement, as if to get out. I was expected to run or apologize. I was not in that mood, and pointing to the ground I suggested: "There is plenty of room." I placed my arms akimbo for the attack. He was armed, of course. He was in Texas. He had come out especially to humble a Negro. He did not get out. He did not get up. As I placed my hands akimbo, his eye flashed toward my right. My first opinion was that he believed my right hand might be nearing a gun. Later I decided that his eye had caught sight of the Phi Beta Kappa Key on my watch fob. He had studied in a northern college. The best I could make of it was, that he conceived the idea that, if he attacked, there would at least be a fight. There was no help for me, and no immediate help for him. He backed his auto, turned about, and quietly withdrew.

But because I knew Texas, I still expected trouble, and I prepared for it: for those colored people had seen his discomfiture, for which he would hardly forgive me. William Tell's worst offense was, that he met the tyrant alone in the woods and the tyrant trembled,—for which the tyrant never forgave Tell.* But to my genuine surprise a few weeks later, when I was in New York, I received a letter from Mrs. Pickens, saying: "Well! A————sent the money."—He never apologized nor explained. But I was to understand by receipt of that money, that the only reason why I was allowed to continue my life on earth, was that this white man had decided that I was right.

So much for the peril of everyday life. In the next chapter we shall relate an incident illustrative of the perils of travel.

---

*William Tell, legendary liberator of Switzerland from Austrian oppression.

THIRTEEN

ARKANSAS TRAVELER

I was to journey back from New York to Texas. In the East I had spoken twenty times in two weeks. I was very tired. I hired a Pullman berth to St. Louis and traveled without incident. Out of deference to the color prejudice of the South I took this northerly route from New York to Texas. I also aimed to leave New York City on an early enough train to reach St. Louis next morning in time to take a daylight ride in Jim Crow from there to Little Rock, Arkansas, where I could stay overnight with my father and then take another daylight ride to Marshall. Most prejudiced white people will never know how many sincere efforts intelligent colored people make to avoid disturbing and irritating contacts, even when the colored people would be entirely within their legal and just rights. But the Republican Club of New York, before which my last address was made, kept me so late that I could only catch a train that brought me to St. Louis next afternoon. That left me one choice among three evil alternatives: to stay that night in St. Louis and the next night in Little Rock, thereby losing another twenty-four hours from school and family; or to sit up a night and a day in the unspeakable torture of the Jim Crow car; or to get a Pullman ticket for the night to Little Rock, and so run the risk of trouble with insane prejudiced people. Having been absent from family and pupils so long, I decided to risk the last named evil.

How could I get a Pullman ticket to a southern point out of St. Louis, where they try to refuse colored people such accommodations even into other parts of Missouri and toward the north? I decided to take Pullman for only the sleeping hours to Little Rock, where early next morning I would enter Jim Crow for the rest of the journey. The problem of getting the ticket was easily solved: I simply went into the colored section of St. Louis and got a white Negro friend to purchase it. For just as we have exhibited at world's fairs the phenomenon of white black-birds, so have we in the United States the verbal contradiction of white black-people, many of them being one hundred per cent black, if you please, in their consciousness. But my success in providing myself with this simple human necessity for sleep and bodily salvation brought me an experience on that train which I shall describe for the information of the incredulous.

As I entered the Pullman car, the conductor took my tickets, looked at them, and jerked them back into my hand with a nervous ostentation which clearly indicated that it was his opinion that I had no right to such accommodations. Then the colored porter took my bags, with a humorous smile playing on his features, and conducted me to my section. The porter was walking on air, seemed tickled to death, and was saying by his actions: "Well, brother, and how on earth did you manage to put it over on them?"

My ticket was secured late and I could get only an upper, so that I knew I had a section mate. I therefore boarded the train early, so as to be first in the section and avoid the appearance of being the aggressor in the scene that was probable. I have noticed that when white people of the South (and some of the North) encounter a black man on a Pullman car leaving, say, St. Louis for Chicago, they behave lawfully, even if unkindly, toward him; but when the same white people encounter a black person on Pullman leaving St. Louis for Arkansas, Cincinnati for Alabama, or Washington for Georgia, they sometimes make an unlawful and an awful scene. So I planned to "get there first" in the section, and not seem to be the active cause of this likely scene. I deposited my luggage in the section and busied myself reading a book. Later I decided to deposit my luggage on my seat, and to sit for the time being in another yet unoccupied section toward the rear, from which vantage point I could observe and see what manner of person might enter to be my section mate.

As I sat in this other section, still reading the book, a seedy-looking white man entered the front door, carrying a small worn and rusty bag. Observing him casually, I thought to myself: "Any kind of white person, of any class, character or grade of intelligence, can buy and claim his accommodations without indirection or embarrassment." Just then I felt, rather than saw, this individual stop short as he was proceeding down the aisle. He had spied me. It was just as when a bull suddenly catches sight of a waving red rag. I continued to read, and was apparently unconscious of his presence. After a few moments of unfriendly staring he went on to his berth, with a recovered air which seemed to say: "Well, so long as you don't get any nearer to me than that, maybe I'll behave." Then as bad luck would have it, he proceeded straight to the section where my coat and bags were located and deposited his satchel. He had the lower berth.

The train had not yet started, so he went on out of the car, as if to cool off a bit from the sudden heat which the sight of me had aroused in him. I concluded that, while he was out, I would get back into the section and wait on the issues of the untoward fates. Other passengers entered, transfixed me with their unwelcoming glances, and then took their seats,—for luckily I was not in their sections. All this I saw, and did not see: I had never ceased to read.

The conductor shouted "All aboard!" and my section mate re-entered. When he espied me where I was now seated, he struck a posture which could be felt in the very air, strode like a colossus toward me, mustering into his actions all the possible expressiveness of resentment, seized his humble-looking bag as if it were the culprit, and walked out to another part of the train, perhaps the smoking room, attracting everybody's eyes, except mine: I continued to read, as if I had seen nothing.

But there was now some tension in my waiting, for I knew well what was going on. It was a long time before the conductor came through (from the direction of the smoking room) to take tickets, and I knew what that meant. As he came to other passengers, he said "Pullman tickets, please!" But when he came to my seat, he said nothing,—simply stopped, stood still. I reached coolly into my left vest pocket, took out my ticket and handed it to him,—not taking my eyes off the passage which I was reading in the book. He took my ticket, examined it painfully, then stood and coughed and moved his feet upon the floor,—then coughed and stirred and stood again. All the while my hand which had handed him the ticket, was poised in the air, elbow resting on seat arm, waiting for him to put back into it my "passenger's check." He wanted me to *say something* or give some sort of evidence that would enable him to size me up or get a judgment of me, so that he would know better how to begin the attack, which I knew he was going to make. I knew what he wanted. He did not get it. I continued to read.

After an age or so he said: "Er—er—is this yo' ticket?"

Then for the first time I turned my face from my book, and looked up at him with an honest puzzling knit upon my brow. I said not a word, but my look said: "Why, man alive! did not I just now hand you that ticket?" He heard the look, and with a little more quandary than at first he resumed: "Well—er—what I meant to say is—er—you can't ride on this ticket: the laws of Arkansas" . . .

I interrupted him with the first words from my mouth: "The laws of Arkansas have nothing to do with the matter. I bought the ticket in Missouri. I am an interstate passenger."

Then in the exasperation of despair he showed his real fangs: "What I mean is, you'll git hurt in this car, an' you better git out o' here while you can!" When I made no response, either by word or movement, he continued to a climax, raising his voice so that every person in the car turned to listen: "You are going to git shot if you stay in here,—you are going to git killed!"—Still I made no response, and still my hand reached for the passenger's portion of my ticket, whereupon he, as if he judged me either hard of hearing or difficult of understanding, reddened and thundered: "I say, you're going to *git hurt*,—you're going to *be killed* if you don't git out!"

As if I had suddenly grasped the idea that he was insisting upon some reply, I said naturally and simply: "Well, I'm sorry!" But I made no move, and my hand continued to reach for my check.

In confusion he wheeled and went back to the smoking room,—and I knew why he had gone. He had not given me my check, and I smelt treachery. But it had been advertised to the whole car that I did actually have a ticket, so I waited quietly—and read.

After a while he returned, and other men came behind him and slid into the seats across the aisle opposite me. My temper had risen and my determination was absolutely fixed, but my self-control was still good. With as little excitement as possible I snapped the fingers of my reaching hand and said: "You forgot to give me my passenger's check." And then he screamed out, again attracting the attention of the whole car: "What! are you going to risk it? These Arkansas fellers are going to shoot yo' head off! Are you going to risk it?"

To this I replied, with as little passion as possible but also loud enough to be heard by the whole car, and uttering my words slowly as if counting them: "I am going to stay right where I am,—and attend to my own business!"—He handed me my check with a jerk and strode forward out of the car with a show of passion and a flood of words, among which could be distinguished: "Shot—killed—head shot off!"

It is an awful feeling: desperation *and* determination. I would have it out at once: I called the porter and told him to make down my berth so that I could retire. As I ascended the ladder, I told him in a low voice to apprise me of any hostile movements towards me, so that I might wake up and do my duty. I was surprised and pleased to hear him reply in a loud voice, that rang of indirect defiance: "I'll do it— you bet I will!"

He had had no chance to express himself previously: he could not interfere or meddle in the conductor's business, and now at his first opportunity he showed up fearless and true. I learned later that he had kept his eye and ear on the whole situation and had resolved to sacrifice his job and any thing else to stand with me, if it came to that.—Your Pullman porter is a wonderful being. He understands. Nobody ever fools the porter. No man in all the world can "size" you quicker. He knows who you are and what you are, be you male or female. Your traveling camouflages are nothing to him. You may fool the ticket agent and the station officers, the trainmen, the conductors and your fellow-passengers, and everybody else except God and the Pullman porter.

My resignation caused me to sleep as much as usual: I had no expectation of seeing the light of day again, so I had nothing to worry about. Worry would be useless, so I slept, with the finger of my right hand coiled over the trigger of a deadly weapon.—Can they who have not had the experience, understand that? I think I would not have gone into this car if I had *known* that it would cost me my life and destroy the life of others. But being in was another thing, and being bullied out was impossible. I remembered my boyhood in Arkansas: that just twenty years before I had defied death there, when an officer had drawn a Colt's pistol to shoot me because I was fighting for respect to my sister,—and I had kept right on fighting.

One thing I felt very keenly conscious of—the lies that would be told by the newspapers next day. After I was mobbed and murdered, I would be accused in the whole civilized press of having attacked everybody in the car,—of having abused, insulted, annoyed. As a fact I had uttered less than a hundred words and had molested nobody. But I could see the headlines: "NEGRO TAKEN FROM PULLMAN CAR AND BURNED IN ARKANSAS." Then there were the details: "Negro, said to have been drunk, got on train and began to use insulting language *to the ladies*. Some of the white men tried to quiet him, when he pulled a gun and shot wildly, wounding two or three people. The conductor wired ahead and a posse met the train. The mob which had gathered at the station, overpowered the officers, and the Negro, fighting madly, was chained to a lamp post, saturated with gasoline"—etc., etc. Then all the hundred million people of the United States, except the few thousands who knew me personally, would have thought that there was at least some truth in the report about my provocative behavior. "It's too bad, of course—I think Negro criminals ought to be executed by law—but then, *what could he expect?*" This would have been the reflection of the innocent.

Fortunately no attack was made on me that night. The paucity of my words and my seeming indifference to the threat of death had evidently puzzled somebody. Next morning, however, the attack was renewed from another flank. I had arisen early and the porter had let me make my toilet in the drawing-room,—still trying to sidestep unreasonable prejudice. In Little Rock I was to get off or go forward into the Jim Crow car, and we were due there at about seven. The train conductor out of St. Louis had evidently not supported the Pullman conductor and the others in their attack on me, but during the night at Bald Knob a new train conductor had got aboard, a real "Arkansas feller." He had heard the awful tidings that I was in Pullman, and had inquired diligently concerning me. He had learned little, for I was an enigma. He therefore took aboard the sheriff of one of the rural counties, stationed the officer in the Jim Crow car, and then came back to the drawing-room, where he tried to irritate me and threatened me with arrest: "I've got a sheriff on this train, an' he says he'll arrest you.— Do you want to be arrested?"

In the bottom of my heart and the center of my soul I had very decided objections to enjoying any such luxury in Arkansas, but I coolly replied "That is for you and the railroad company to decide. All I wanted was *a rest* on this car last night. *The rest* is up to you." He visibly weakened a bit, and I think he mistook my words *a rest* for the word *arrest*, and began to guess that maybe I was some decoy to make a federal case against the railroad.

As we were nearing Little Rock, and not wanting to have to get off the train, so that whatever happened to me would burden the railroad with some responsibility, I called the porter to take my bags and lead me forward into the Jim Crow car. The Arkansas conductor followed us, nagging and shouting: "You had no business in hyeah!" as if trying to draw some further remark from me. In the Jim Crow car was the county sheriff, six feet tall, heavy, red, rough, booted. As I passed in without apparent concern, he addressed no word to me, but remarked defiantly over my shoulder to the conductor who was following me: "Wa-al, I'll arrest him, an' turn him over to the officers in Little Rock."

The sheriff then glared at me, evidently expecting me to answer or acknowledge this indirect statement. I gave neither word nor sign. Passing him in the aisle I took a seat and began to write letters on the back of my suitcase. The conductor and the officer took their seats in Jim Crow, discussed and puzzled over the mystery of me and the greater mystery of the race question. The conductor evidently did not feel sure that it was best to insist upon arrest. When we reached Little Rock, the giant sheriff got up, went to the car door, wheeled around and ran me through with bayonet glances. I looked at him with a "poker face," an absence of all emotion. Then he went out on the station platform, came up beside the window where I sat, and thrust at me the same hostile looks. I looked out at him and the passers-by and the trunks and trucks and other scenery with the same interest. Then slowly the boots carried him up the station steps, as he shot back a single glance. My train pulled out for Texas.

Protest to the railroad or Pullman officers in such a case usually means nothing to anybody. They will not incriminate themselves. Letters get lost. If it be registered to them, one may receive a polite reply, saying: "The matter will be investigated." That is the end of the matter.

I had another odd, but pleasant, experience before I reached Texas. Suddenly and unexpectedly I encountered the man who had "pitched headin'" to me nearly twenty years before, and who had tried his best to knock my head off with the green oak slabs. We had stopped at a little railway station in southern Arkansas, and I heard outside a voice in command of a gang of Negro railroad workmen who were boarding the train. Strange that, though I could not see the speaker, I recognized instantly the voice of "Dink" Jeter,—stranger still, because I had heard from the mouth of one of his relatives eleven years before, that he was dead, cut to death in a brawl, and I had never heard anything to the contrary. And yet the moment I heard him speak, out in the early night where I could see neither his face nor his figure, I did not think that it was a voice *like his*,—I knew that it was *his* voice and that he was alive.

When he came into the car, I waited, but he did not recognize me until I made myself known. I had changed more; he was still at twenty years ago. I have never in all my life been happier at meeting a person whom I had known years before, and no such person has ever seemed happier to see me again. This fellow, who had done his uttermost to kill or maim me when I was a child, now put his arms about me, hugged me dramatically and called out to the bewildered railroad hands: "See this boy! I been knowin' him all his life,—this the bes' boy in the whole worl'." This very brutal and very human man, was extravagant in his praises. Nearly a generation before he had used all his demon cunning, endeavoring to catch me off my guard and at least injure me seriously. He asked a thousand questions, simple questions. Perhaps he admired the eternal vigilance with which I had saved myself from him. When he reached his destination, I was loth to part with him. Years ago I had never quite felt that he was a real personal enemy and had felt that he was acting out the natural resentment of the older workmen, who must have regarded me as something of a "scab" for "layin' headin' " at seventy-five cents a day, while grown men wanted a dollar.

This chance meeting with "Dink" Jeter was a test for the sentiment which I had expressed years before, when I thought he was dead: that I could never feel hatred or resentment toward the man, and that as I looked back, he seemed to be one of my appointed teachers who trained me in the art of vigilant self-defense. All summer he had attacked; all summer I had defended.—To me he had been dead for years. He reappeared like a ghost. But for the other men about, I might have regarded him as an apparition. Even now his resurrection seems like a dream.

In 1915 Morgan College,* in Baltimore, Maryland, elected me as dean. The position offered many advantages over my situation in Texas, especially for the education of our children. I therefore moved to Baltimore, to the old site of Morgan College at the corner of Fulton and Edmondson Avenues. The president was the Rev. Dr. John Oakley Spencer. The teachers were white and colored. It was a new departure to have a colored man for dean.

---

*Morgan College, now Morgan State University, in Baltimore, Maryland, originated in 1867 as a school for the training of black ministers. In the 1890s the Methodist Episcopal Church expanded the school's program, making it a college emphasizing the education of blacks for careers in public school teaching.

FOURTEEN

MORGAN COLLEGE
AND AFTER

In 1915, as I was on my way from Texas to Maryland, Selma University, an institution in Alabama for the education of colored youth, conferred upon me the degree of Literarum Doctor. In December of that year President Spencer had me formally installed as Dean of Morgan College, with the presence and participation of many leaders of education, including the governor, the state superintendent of education and educators from neighboring States.

Morgan College was at that time a small institution, physically, because it had no ground on which to grow. It was smothered in the heart of Baltimore. But it had two branch schools, one at Princess Anne, Maryland, and the other at Lynchburg, Virginia. The branch schools were preparatory in grade, and many of their graduates would enter Morgan College proper for further study.

In 1917 our country entered the World War. As always, the great question—"What shall we do with the Negro?"—immediately arose. It was plain to everybody that the Negro would have to be in the army. The white man may not need the Negro soldier in the dress-parade days of peace, but "black troops" have always been very useful and very welcome in the days of actual war. There was no debate worth considering on that point. But at first no provision was made for the Negro to be anything but a private. He was not even admitted to camps like Plattsburg. Some of us saw that it would be a calamity to the Negro race in America, and a very uncomfortable thing for the Negro soldier in the army, if he got in only as private.

A people situated like the American Negro will often find itself between the horns of dilemma, face to face with a choice of evils: now there was racial segregation on the one horn, and on the other the most awful oppression at the bottom of the military establishment. At the risk, therefore, of the undoubted evil and wrong of segregation, some of us advocated an officers' training camp for Negroes and finally secured one at Fort Des Moines, Iowa. At first Dr. Joel E. Spingarn, a Jewish gentleman of New York City and later a major in the army overseas,* and I were the only persons well known to colored Americans, who ventured to make a choice in this dilemma. Colored people were so set against segregation that, naturally, for the moment they failed to see that segregation was, under the circumstances, the lesser evil of the two. The greater evil would have been to have hundreds of thousands of Negro soldiers in the army with no Negro officers. "A private has no rights which an officer is bound to respect."** Mr. Spingarn and I therefore advocated a camp for prospective Negro officers, not as an ideal democratic arrangement but as the better choice of the evils. It would not make the world safe for democracy, but it would make the United States army much less dangerous for the Negro. We took the matter first before the student body of the largest Negro college, Howard University, in Washington. The bright and aggressive young men caught the idea at once, organized a students' committee which ramified to all other Negro institutions, and did not cease to annoy the War Department until the Fort Des Moines Training Camp was an accomplished fact.

Those who did not see at first, saw later: that while you are fighting for an ideal, you must live in the real. Mr. Spingarn and I had always stimulated, encouraged and led colored Americans to oppose public segregation. That is a sound principle and an ultimate aim. But the policy of the present is always determined, by those who are wise, with a consideration of present circumstances. If a man lived in a district infested by wild beasts, his *ideal* might be: a district-free-from-wild-beasts. But it would hardly behoove him to walk abroad unarmed and careless, as if the ideal were a fact. Before the war was a year old, the wisdom of this training camp was recognized so unanimously that people actually forgot how alone and abused Major Spingarn and I were when we fought the first battles of the idea.

---

*Joel E. Spingarn (1875–1939), literary critic and political activist, was elected chairman of the board of directors of the NAACP in 1914.
**In this quotation Pickens parodies the infamous language of the U.S. Supreme Court's Dred Scott decision of 1857, in which Chief Justice Roger B. Taney concluded that African Americans "had no rights which the white man was bound to respect."

Morgan College needed a new site. President Spencer had been trying for years to secure one. Finally a site of more than eighty acres, with a few stone buildings convertible to school uses, was secured far out on Hillen Road but within the corporate limits of Baltimore. It would make a story by itself to recite how much opposition developed to the location of a Negro college. White people who lived miles from the proposed site, were duped by real estate companies and other selfish interests into opposition to the institution. Circulars were passed around saying that chicken thieves, criminals and rapists were coming into the neighborhood,—that is, a Negro Christian College, of the best boys and girls of the state. Half of the trustee board of Morgan College were white men, who knew well the character of the institution and its need, and who fought for it. Among these was the president of the board, Dr. John F. Goucher, founder and president emeritus of Goucher College for white girls. The school was not without friends among other whites who knew its history, and who knew human nature. Opposition was finally overcome, and we located the school on one of the best university sites in the whole country.

For three years I had been dean of the college. When we moved to the new site in 1918, I was made vice-president. In this same year Wiley University, where I had previously worked in Texas, gave me the degree of Legum Doctor (LL.D.).

The reader of this story may have a sense or suspicion of interesting details left out. A colored American's life is full of human-interest vicissitudes. I have aimed to give a suggestion of the life I have lived so far. During all my years of teaching, the call of the general public for me as a lecturer continued to be persistent, as it had been since my pupil days. While working for Morgan College, I usually spent my thirty days of vacation on a trip from coast to coast, speaking to various audiences of white and colored Americans. I also accepted occasional week-end engagements.

I had appeared at many meetings of the National Association for the Advancement of Colored People and its branches. Since a very few years after the Association was formed, there had been suggestions, and occasional negotiations, to have me spend all my time in the national work for colored people. Finally on February 1, 1920, I accepted a position as Field Secretary of the organization. In June, when the schools attended by our children had closed in Baltimore, my family moved to New York. As I write, William, Jr., has graduated from high school, Harriet Ida is in the second year of high school, and Ruby Annie is in the seventh year at grammar school. *Fugit tempus.*

And for nearly eighteen years Mrs. Pickens has made the place wherever we lived a wonderful home for the children and for me.—The world still seems good, not all good, but altogether interesting, and always improving.

January, 1923.

WILLIAM PICKENS, born in 1881, was the sixth of ten children and the first son born to Jacob and Fannie Pickens, former slaves who gained their freedom after the fall of the Confederacy in 1865. A Phi Beta Kappa graduate of Yale, he became a nationally recognized African American leader, one of the half-dozen best-known black men of his time.

WILLIAM L. ANDREWS is Joyce and Elizabeth Hall Professor of American Literature at the University of Kansas. He is the author of *To Tell a Free Story: The First Century of Afro-American Autobiography, 1760–1865* and the editor of a number of books on autobiography, including *Sisters of the Spirit: Three Black Women's Autobiographies of the Nineteenth Century.*